THE WORLD
FOOD CRISIS

Edited by Herbert L. Marx, Jr.

THE REFERENCE SHELF
Volume 47   Number 6

THE H. W. WILSON COMPANY   •   New York   •   1975

THE REFERENCE SHELF

The books in this series contain reprints of articles, excerpts from books, and addresses on current issues and social trends in the United States and other countries. There are six separately bound numbers in each volume, all of which are generally published in the same calendar year. One number is a collection of recent speeches; each of the others is devoted to a single subject and gives background information and discussion from various points of view, concluding with a comprehensive bibliography. Books in the series may be purchased individually or on subscription.

Library of Congress Cataloging in Publication Data
Main entry under title:

World food crisis.

(The Reference shelf ; v. 47, no. 6)
Bibliography: p.
SUMMARY: Articles, addresses, and excerpts from books explore the world's food crisis, means of increasing food supply, interrelation between population and food supply, and the role of the United States and United Nations with special reference to the 1974 World Food Conference.
1. Food supply. 2. Population. 3. Economic assistance. [1. Food supply. 2. Population. 3. Economic assistance] I. Marx, Herbert L. II. Series.

HD9000.5.W57   338.1'9   75-35642
ISBN 0-8242-0574-X

PREFACE

Care must be exercised in pasting the popular label of crisis on the worsening world food situation, which has so widely varying effects in different places. To the American homemaker, the "crisis" may mean only the rising cost of meat and other food staples, which creates havoc with the family budget and results possibly in a significant change in diet to accommodate inflation. For some nations the food situation may mean economic dislocation, but not necessarily deprivation: the USSR, for example, during its severe wheat shortage of 1972, required massive imports. But for regions of the world temporarily or chronically beset by drought, deleterious climate change, and resulting crop failure, the situation is literally one of life and death: India, for example, faces the imminent or actual failure of the vital balance between the amount of food available and the number of mouths to be fed—in short, famine.

Yet, in the purest sense of the word, crisis means a turning point—frequently from bad to good. In that semantic context, it does seem appropriate to describe the world food situation as a crisis, for we are at the point where we can—must—resolve the complexities of the problem or face barely imaginable consequences.

Famine, starvation, natural disaster, and the dislocations and deprivations of war have always been with us. There is little startlingly new on this front, even if the locale of danger and suffering changes from time to time. Improvement in agricultural techniques—the broadening of such knowledge, and its ever-widening application—has been and continues to be part of human progress. Yet there are other factors which are cumulative and increasingly important. One is the continuous rise in world population. Another is the fact that in many nations—the United States in particular—steadily rising living standards have led to a greater per capita consumption of food. What was once considered an adequate diet is no longer sufficient amid constantly rising expectations. Thus even greater disparities grow between the "have" and the "have not" nations.

Within these dimensions, the 1970s are marked by a world food crisis. What are its characteristics and background, and what can be done about it? To explore these questions is the purpose of this volume.

The selections herein are principally directed at the world situation. Within the United States there are, of course, many problems of food production, distribution, and consumption. Incentives and protection for American farmers are a continuing cause of congressional debate. From the federal government, nearly 20 million Americans receive food stamps—financial aid to help feed those with insufficient means to provide for themselves. Malnutrition affects American children in many regions; such suffering is not confined to distant lands. The price of food—and therefore, for some, its availability—has been one of the leading elements of the current economic inflation. But these are all matters of economic and political policy—not basically the question of insufficient food supply for the nation as a whole —and beyond the parameters of this book.

Section I of this volume presents a broad view of the world food situation, and in Section II particular famine crisis points are more closely examined. Section III deals with plans and achievements to increase food supply, especially in areas which are not self-sufficient.

Will expansion of food supplies suffice? In Section IV the interrelation between population growth and food supply is discussed from widely varying angles.

Sections V and VI describe the respective roles of the American government and the United Nations, with special reference to the achievements of the 1974 World Food Conference, held at US urging and under UN auspices. Section VII takes a look to the future to see what can and should be accomplished in the years ahead.

The editor expresses sincere appreciation to the organizations, publishers, publications, and authors who have granted permission to include the materials which make up this volume. Special acknowledgment is also made to Professor Robert E. Huke, chairman, geography department, Dartmouth College; John T. Thacher, assistant executive director, CARE; and Norman R. Michie, information liaison officer, Food and Agriculture Organization of the United Nations, for providing information and suggestions on many helpful sources in the preparation of this volume.

HERBERT L. MARX, JR.

October 1975

CONTENTS

I. FOOD: CHALLENGE OF THE SEVENTIES

EDITOR'S INTRODUCTION

How can the world food crisis be measured? It ebbs and flows with climatic and economic conditions. It cannot be surveyed as one would the relative strengths of opposing military forces. It does not necessarily stay in one place. This introductory section attempts to apply some yardsticks to what is almost certain to be the most critical human problem of the 1970s.

Lester R. Brown, a leading world expert on food supply, begins this study with a gloomy overall view of food scarcity around the globe. This is followed by a similar broad analysis by the authoritative Economic Research Service of the United States Department of Agriculture.

In the United States greater consideration is given to the rising prices of food than to its scarcity. Lawrence A. Mayer of *Fortune* reviews the changing rank of food in the consumer's over-all budget.

The availability of fertilizer could readily make the difference between food abundance and scarcity, and D. L. McCune of the Tennessee Valley Authority describes the near-term outlook in this phase of the problem. William A. Hewitt, chief executive of an agricultural machinery company, takes a more optimistic view of world food supply prospects in the next article, but Boyce Rensberger, of the New York *Times*, reminds us of the ever-changing, ever-present nature of the crisis.

AN EMERGING CHRONIC GLOBAL SCARCITY [1]

During the 1960s, the world food problem was perceived as a food/population problem centered on the developing countries, a race between food and people. At the end of each year, observers anxiously compared rates of increase in food production with those of population growth to see if any progress was being made. Throughout most of the decade it was nip and tuck. During the 1970s, rapid global population growth continues to generate demand for more food, but, in addition, rising affluence is emerging as a major new claimant on the world's food resources. Thus there are now two important sources of growth in world demand for food.

Worldwide, population growth is still the dominant source of expanding demand for food. With world population expanding at nearly 2 percent per year, merely maintaining current per capita consumption levels will require a doubling of food production in little more than a generation.

Throughout the poor countries, population growth accounts for most of the year-to-year growth in the demand for food. At best, only very limited progress is being made in raising per capita consumption. In the more affluent countries, on the other hand, rising incomes account for most of the growth in the demand for food.

As the world demand for food climbs, constraints on efforts to further expand food production become increasingly apparent. The primary means available for expanding supplies fall into two categories: either increasing the amount of land under cultivation, or raising yields on existing cropland through intensified use of water, fertilizers, and energy. We face problems in the needed expansion of each of these physical resources.

[1] From address by Lester R. Brown, senior fellow, Overseas Development Council, at Midwest Conference on Food Policy, June 7, 1974. In *Between You and Hunger*, ed. by Milton D. Hakel. Minnesota Farmers Union. 1275 University Ave. St. Paul, Minn. 55104. '74. p 32-4. Reprinted by permission.

The traditional approach to increasing production—expanding the area under cultivation—has only limited potential for the future. Some parts of the world actually face a net reduction in agricultural land because of the growth in competing uses, such as industrial development, recreation, transportation, and residential development. Few countries have well-defined land use policies that protect land from other uses. In the United States, farmland has been used indiscriminately for other purposes with little thought devoted to the possible long-term consequences. Some more densely populated countries, for example Japan and several Western European countries, have used decreasing amounts of land for crop production in the past few decades. Other parts of the world, including particularly the Indian subcontinent, the Middle East, North and sub-Saharan Africa, the Caribbean, Central America, and the Andean countries, are losing disturbingly large acreages of cropland each year because of severe erosion.

The availability of water for agricultural purposes will be particularly critical for food production in the future. In many regions of the world, fertile agricultural land would be available if water could be found to make it productive. But most of the rivers that lend themselves to damming and to irrigation already have been developed. The expansion of irrigated area is likely to slow down as we run out of easy opportunities to continue expanding. Future efforts to expand fresh water supplies for agricultural purposes increasingly will focus on such techniques as the diversion of rivers (as in the Soviet Union today), desalting sea water, and the manipulation of rainfall patterns to increase the share of rain falling over moisture-deficient agricultural areas.

In many developing countries, intensification of agricultural production on the existing cultivated area will require a severalfold increase in energy supplies. With world energy prices increasing rapidly, the costs of intensifying food production will rise commensurately. In countries (such as the United States) that are already engaged in agriculture requiring large energy inputs, high energy prices and the possibility of fuel rationing may hold down future production.

In addition to arable land, fresh water, and energy, fertilizer is in short supply, and the outlook in this case, too, is higher prices.

By early 1974, there were signs that many nations—including some very populous ones, such as India, Indonesia, Pakistan, and the Philippines—would be unable to obtain the needed amounts of fertilizer regardless of price.

At a time when rising affluence is beginning to manifest itself in the form of rapidly growing demand for high quality protein, we suddenly find ourselves in difficulty in our efforts to rapidly expand supplies of three major protein sources—beef, soybeans, and fish. Two major constraints are operative in the case of beef. Agricultural scientists have not been able to devise any commercially satisfactory means of getting more than one calf per cow per year. For every animal that goes into the beef production process, one adult animal must be fed and otherwise maintained for a full year. There does not appear to be any prospect of an imminent breakthrough on this front.

The other constraint of beef production is good grassland. The grazing capacity of much of the world's pastureland is now almost fully utilized. This is true, for example, in much of the US Great Plains area, in sub-Saharan Africa, and in parts of Australia. There are opportunities for using improved grasses and for improved range management, but these are limited and slow to be realized.

A second potentially serious constraint on efforts to expand supplies of high-quality protein is the inability of scientists to achieve a breakthrough in per acre yields of soybeans.

In the United States, which now produces two thirds of the world's soybean crop and supplies more than four fifths of all soybeans entering the world market, soybean yields per acre have increased by about 1 percent per year.

The growing demand for food is putting more pressure on the food producing ecosystem in many parts of the world than it can withstand. One dramatic example is the anchovy fishery off the western coast of Latin America. During the early seventies this vast fishery accounted for one fifth of the global fish catch. During late 1972 and throughout much of 1973 the anchovies seemingly disappeared from the traditional offshore fishing areas. This did not cause a great deal of alarm since a slight shift in the Humboldt current and the change in temperature of a few degrees had caused the anchovies to move away at least temporarily before.

There is now growing evidence that the very heavy offtake from the anchovy fishery ranging from 10 to 12 million tons in the late sixties and early seventies may have exceeded the capacity of the fishery to regenerate itself. Overfishing may have seriously damaged the anchovy fishery. If so, it may take years before it can recover to its full productive capacity, assuming it is given the opportunity to do so.

A second example of ecological overstress, which is diminishing the earth's food producing capacity, is now all too evident in the Sahel, just south of the Sahara in Africa. [See articles on the Sahel in Section II, below.]

There is a much more basic problem in the Sahel. Over the past thirty-five years, human and livestock populations along the sub-Saharan fringe have increased rapidly, in some areas nearly doubling during this period. As the human and livestock populations multiply, they put more pressure on the ecosystem than it can withstand. The result is overgrazing, deforestation, and overall denudation of the land.

As a result of this denudation and deforestation, the Sahara desert has begun to move southward at an accelerated rate all along the 3,500 mile southern fringe, stretching from Senegal to northern Ethiopia. A United States Govern-

ment study indicates the desert is moving southward at up
to thirty miles per year, depending on where it is measured.

As the desert moves southward, human and livestock
population retreat before it. The result is ever-greater pressure on the fringe area. This in turn contributes to the
denudation and deforestation, setting in process a self-rein-
forcing cycle.

The green revolution does not represent a solution to
the food problem; rather, it is a means of buying time, perhaps an additional fifteen or twenty years during which the
brakes can be applied to population growth. [See Section
III, The Green Revolution—and Beyond, below.]

Close to a decade has now passed since the launching of
the green revolution, but success stories in national family
planning programs in the poor nations are all too few.
Among the population giants of Asia, the People's Republic of China appears to be substantially reducing its birth
rates, but reductions in India, Indonesia, Pakistan, and
Bangladesh are minimal. The futility of relying on the new
agricultural technologies is evident in Mexico, the country
where the green revolution first began. Fifteen years of
dramatic advances in wheat production made Mexico a net
exporter of cereals in the late sixties, but a population
growth rate among the highest in the world has converted
Mexico into an importer of food. [See "Borlaug and the
Green Revolution," in Section III, below.]

The period since World War II has been characterized
by excess capacity in world agriculture, much of it concentrated in the United States. In many ways the world was
fortunate to have, in effect, two major food reserves during
this period. One was in the form of grain reserves in the
principal exporting countries and the other in the form of
reserve cropland, virtually all of which was land idled under
farm programs in the United States.

Grain reserves, including substantial quantities of both
foodgrains and feedgrains, are most commonly measured in
terms of carryover stocks—the amount in storage at the time

the new crop begins to come in. World carryover stocks are concentrated in a few of the principal exporting countries —namely the United States, Canada, Australia, and Argentina.

Since 1960, world grain reserves have fluctuated from a high of 155 million metric tons to a low of about 100 million metric tons. When these reserves drop to 100 million tons, severe shortages and strong upward price pressures develop. Although 100 million tons appears to be an enormous quantity of grain, it represents a mere 8 percent of annual world grain consumption, or less than one month's needs— an uncomfortably small working reserve and a perilously thin buffer against the vagaries of weather or plant diseases. As world consumption expands by some 2.5 percent annually, so should the size of working reserves, but over the past two decades reserves have dwindled while consumption has continued to climb.

The extent of global vulnerability is particularly underlined by examining the degree of global dependence on North America for exportable food supplies. Over the past generation the United States has achieved a unique position as a supplier of food to the rest of the world. Before World War II both Latin America, importantly Argentina, and North America (United States and Canada) were major exporters of grain. During the late thirties net grain exports from Latin America were substantially above those of North America. Since then, however, the combination of the population explosion and the slowness of most Latin American governments to reform and modernize agriculture have eliminated the net export surplus. With few exceptions, Latin American countries are now food importers.

At a time when dependence of the rest of the world on North American food exports is increasing so dramatically, there is also a growing awareness that this extreme dependence leaves the world in a very dangerous position in the event of adverse crop years in North America. Both the

United States and Canada are affected by the same climatic cycles.

Considerable evidence has now been accumulated indicating that North America has been subject to recurrent clusters of drought years roughly every twenty years. The cyclical drought phenomenon has now been established as far back as the Civil War when data were first collected on rainfall.

The most recent drought, occurring in the early fifties, was rather modest. The preceding one occurring in the early thirties was particularly severe, giving rise to the dust bowl era in the United States.

If the United States experiences another stretch of drought years, quite possibly during the current decade, its impact on production will not likely be as great as during the thirties due to improved soil management and water conservation practices. But even a modest decline in production, given the rapid growth in global demand and extreme world dependence on North America's exportable margin of food, would create a very dangerous situation. It would send shock waves throughout the world triggering intense competition for available food supplies.

High food prices and shortages are an inconvenience for the more affluent societies and individuals, but the poor nations, and the poor within nations, are in an especially dangerous predicament. When global reserve stocks are low, the capacity of the international community to respond to emergencies such as droughts or crop failures with food aid is greatly diminished. At the same time, high prices may keep needed food out of the reach of poor nations and individuals.

When one spends about 80 percent of one's income on food, as does a sizable segment of mankind, a doubling in the price of wheat or rice cannot possibly be offset by increased expenditures. It can only drive a subsistence diet below the subsistence or survival level.

The global food outlook calls for serious consideration of the creation of an internationally managed food reserve system. [See "A World Food Policy" and "A Bold Plan," in Section VII, below.] Just as the US dollar can no longer serve as the foundation of the international monetary system, so US agriculture may no longer have sufficient excess capacity to ensure reasonable stability in the world food economy over a multi-year period.

One of the most immediate means of expanding the food supply is to return the idled US cropland to production, a process already in motion. Over the longer run, however, the greatest opportunities lie in the developing countries, where the world's greatest reservoir of unexploited food potential is located.

In those countries having the appropriate economic incentives, fertilizer, water, and other required agricultural inputs and supporting institutions, the introduction of new wheat and rice varieties has increased production substantially. But the recent jump in per acre yields in many developing countries appears dramatic largely because their yields traditionally have been so low relative to the potential. Today rice yields per acre in India and Nigeria still average only one third those of Japan; corn yields in Thailand and Brazil are less than one third those of the United States. Large increases in food supply are possible in these countries at far less cost than in agriculturally advanced nations if farmers are given the necessary economic incentives and have access to the requisite inputs.

The prospect of an emerging chronic global scarcity of food as a result of growing pressures on available food resources underlines the need to stabilize and eventually halt population growth in as short a period of time as possible. One can conceive of this occurring in the industrial countries given recent demographic trends, particularly if national governments put their minds to it.

In the poor countries, however, it will be much more difficult to achieve population stability within an acceptable time frame, at least as things are going now. For one thing the historical record indicates that birth rates do not usually decline unless certain basic social needs are satisfied—a reasonable standard of living, an assured food supply, a reduced infant mortality rate, literacy, and health services—providing the basic motivation for smaller families.

In short, it is in the self-interest of affluent societies to launch a major additional effort directed at helping developing countries to step up food production and generally accelerate the development of the rural areas, which contain the great majority of the world's people and most of the very poor. This effort would not only increase food production at a relatively low cost, but would also meet the basic social needs of people throughout the world. The latter is a prerequisite in lowering birth rates.

Population-induced pressures on the global food supply will continue to increase if substantial economic and social progress is not made. A greatly expanded program to make family planning services available to all who desire them, in rich and poor nations, will be a necessary but not a sufficient prerequisite to breaking the dismal cycle of ten millenia in which increased food production has always been consumed by an ever-expanding number of mouths to feed, leaving much of mankind hungry. [See Section IV, Food Supply vs. Population, below.]

THE WORLD SITUATION TODAY [2]

Every man, woman and child has the inalienable right to be free from hunger and malnutrition in order to develop fully and maintain their physical and mental facilities. Society today already possesses sufficient resources, organizational ability, and technology and hence the competence to achieve this objective. Accordingly, the eradication of hunger is a common objective of all the countries of the international community, especially of the developed countries and others in a position to help.

[2] From *Summary of the World Food Situation and Prospects to 1985*. Based on *The World Food Situation and Prospects to 1985*. (Foreign Agricultural Economic Report no 98) United States Department of Agriculture. Economic Research Service. Washington, D.C. 20250. '75. p 1-4.

This statement was part of the *Universal Declaration on the Eradication of Hunger* issued at the Third World Food Conference, held in Rome . . . November [1974] and attended by representatives of 130 countries. [See "The Eradication of Hunger," in Section VI, below.] The Conference reflected widespread anxiety about the world's ability to feed its growing population. In 1972, the world food situation had been transformed from one of food surpluses and low prices to one of relative food scarcity and high prices. This rapid reversal has raised again a wave of widespread food-population pessimism similar to that which has swept over the world several times since Thomas Malthus wrote his influential essay in 1798. [See "The Malthusian Theory," in Section IV, below.]

The Economic Research Service (ERS) [of the United States Department of Agriculture] agrees with the Declaration's view that the world does have the basic resources and technology to produce enough food to eliminate hunger. The factors that have given rise to the present widespread critical shortages of food in the world are largely transitory, and given normal weather conditions, can be corrected by intelligent and humane policies.

Major problems must be solved, however, and many of them are not self-correcting. Among the most pressing are:
- □ transferring food from the developed food-exporting countries to the food-deficit developing countries (without preventing needed increases in food production in these countries)
- □ providing for emergency disaster and famine relief
- □ achieving an acceptable degree of stability of world food prices
- □ finding the proper combination of techniques and policies to bring about a substantial improvement in food production and distribution in developing countries

The poor countries that rely on imported grain and fertilizer were the most adversely affected by the food shortages

that prevailed in 1972–74. Any serious decline in their food
production or in general world crop conditions in 1975 or
1976 could have serious consequences requiring emergency
measures beyond those already adopted or now being discussed. Even in the longer run, substantial malnutrition will
probably persist among low-income groups in the less pros-
perous developing countries, unless much greater efforts are
made to produce more food in those countries and distribute
it more equally. Special national and international nutritional programs will continue to be necessary to help those
most seriously threatened by food shortages.

Food Production Trends

The vulnerability of the world to the disruption in food
supply in 1972–74 was influenced by how production and
consumption had developed over the previous two decades
and how governments had responded. Three trends were
especially important: the increasing gap between food production and food needs in developing countries; sporadic
but growing grain imports of the centrally planned economies; and persistent food surpluses in some developed
countries.

From 1954 to 1973 world food production increased
faster than population—production at 2.8 percent annually
and population at 2.0 percent. In these two decades, food
production on a global basis declined only once—in 1972.
The 1954–73 trend rate of growth in total food production
was slightly higher in the developing countries than in the
developed countries. But because of sharply different population growth rates, food production *per capita* rose at an
annual trend rate of only 0.4 percent in the developing
countries, compared with 1.5 percent in the developed
countries. The developing countries (including Asian centrally planned economies) now account for 86 percent of the
world's annual population increase—61 million out of the
70.5 million annual increase in 1973.

Grain production in 1972, however, dropped by 35 million tons, an amount about equal to one year's average annual growth. Grain is the most important single component of the world's food supply and accounts for between 30 and 70 percent of the value of food production in all world regions. It is the major source of food for many of the world's poorest people, supplying 60 to 75 percent of the total calories many of them consume. However, in many developed countries, more grain is fed to livestock than is consumed directly as grain products.

During the late 1960s and early 1970s, the developed grain-exporting countries were restricting grain production in an effort to reduce surplus stocks. Prices of grain and many food and farm products were at low levels. Overcapacity in the fertilizer industry caused low prices of fertilizer during these years. The world seemed to have plentiful, inexpensive supplies of food and of the inputs to produce food.

The large drop in 1972 grain production, which was caused by unfavorable weather in the Soviet Union, India, Australia, Sahelian Africa, and Southeast Asia, was a major factor triggering the recent situation of food shortages and high food prices. But other important developments were the large Soviet grain purchases [from the United States], very rapid economic growth around the world in 1972 and 1973 (which generated greater demand for food), reduced grain reserves, inflation and monetary instability, speculation in commodities, and the effects of the energy crisis. World food production rose substantially in 1973, but not enough to rebuild stocks. Total world production declined slightly again in 1974, primarily because of disappointing weather in the United States, Canada, the Soviet Union, and South Asia.

The recent increases in the prices of food, petroleum, and other commodities were exceptionally large and had exceptional causes. But some adjustments were necessary to reorient priorities with respect to resource use. Between 1969 and 1974, the world consumed more food than was being produced and was able to supply part of the needs by drawing down stocks. Higher food prices are now stimulating more food production. Higher fertilizer prices are stimulating expansion of the fertilizer industry. Higher grain prices are reducing grain used for livestock feed. Higher petroleum costs are causing a search for other energy sources and causing a different attitude toward energy use.

Malnutrition and Poverty

The United Nations has estimated that about 460 million people are malnourished. Malnutrition is primarily a function of poverty. Most of the world's malnourished live in the developing countries—in the Far East and Africa. The UN estimates that between one fifth and one third of all people living in the Far East (excluding Communist Asia), the Near East, and Africa have an insufficient food supply, compared with only 3 percent in the developed countries.

Within households in these regions, when food shortages are especially acute, the women and children are often the most deprived. Children's malnutrition is also affected by their inability to ingest sufficient food when starchy foods are the main staple. The UN has estimated that one half of the young children in the developing countries may suffer in varying degrees from inadequate nutrition.

How much would it take to feed the world's malnourished? Cereals alone could conceivably supply the calories and much of the protein needed by the world's malnourished people. About 0.15 kilograms daily of wheat, rice, corn, sorghum, or millet would provide 500 calories. If the estimated 460 million malnourished people in the world were each provided daily with additional grain equal to 500 calories, much of the world malnutrition would be alleviated. On an annual basis, about 25 million tons of cereal would be needed, an increase of only about 2 percent in average annual world cereal production. The world could rather easily produce 2 percent more grain. The most difficult problems are not those of increasing production of food, but of distributing it to all those who need it.

THE END OF CHEAP FOOD IN AMERICA [3]

The idea of a bounteous American food supply, which goes back to the first Thanksgiving Day, some 350 years ago, has rather suddenly been called into question. . . .

In the years when they took cheap food for granted, Americans could also assume that the trend of food spending could be pretty much taken for granted by anyone making general economic forecasts. Housing, capital goods, defense, inventories—these were the dynamic sectors of the economy, where sizable swings had major impacts on economic growth. But food spending, whose magnitude is about equal to spending on capital goods . . . , could nevertheless be viewed as a "given": its total in any one year could be predicted fairly readily, as could the proportion of total consumer income spent on food. (The proportion declined steadily, from around 20 percent in 1960 to around 16 percent nowadays.) . . .

The short-term outlook for US food prices is not bad. Our prices are affected by worldwide currents of supply and demand, and right now world food supplies are increasing again. . . .

Plenty of Reasons to Be Concerned

And yet a question remains about the long-term implications of . . . [1973s] explosion in food prices. It is possible that the soaring prices were the result of a number of special, nonrecurring circumstances; it is also possible that those prices were the harbinger of a new era. It is at least clear that the United States, which is by a wide margin the major food exporter, cannot be insulated from price pres-

[3] From "We Can't Take Food for Granted Anymore," by Lawrence A. Mayer, member, board of editors, *Fortune*. *Fortune*. 89:84-9+. F. '74. Reprinted from the February 1974 issue of *Fortune* magazine by special permission; © 1974 Time Inc.

sures in other countries. In a world where many nations are increasingly dependent on others for food, where the less developed nations barely produce enough food to keep pace with population growth, and where reserve stocks will be inadequate if harvests turn poor again, there are plenty of reasons to be concerned about price pressures. . . .

The trouble seems to have started with the poor 1972 rice crop. Rice production was off by 5 percent, world rice exports fell by 12 percent, and by late 1973 the world price of rice was up about 150 percent. The shortfalls in the supply of rice shifted some demand to wheat—but wheat too came up short in many countries.

It is a fact of the world's agricultural economy that a relatively small change in output and trade can generate a relatively large change in price. The reason is that a shortfall in production means that additional supplies must come from reserves, and world reserves for most foods are badly distributed; grains constitute the basic world food supplies, and the United States and Canada have traditionally held by far the largest stockpiles.

Enough Wheat for Four Weeks

The recent history of wheat is a prime illustration of the relationships between output and price changes. World output dropped 3 percent in 1972. Exports, principally from the United States, increased about 30 percent to make up for the shortfall. The powerful export demand for wheat depleted existing stockpiles, which declined 40 percent worldwide. As this drawdown in stocks became apparent, the price of wheat in world markets started to soar. So thin was the supply in 1973, according to a report by the Food and Agriculture Organization [FAO] of the United Nations, that wheat reserves in exporting countries were down to a level representing only about four weeks of world consumption.

Another piece of bad luck in both 1972 and 1973 was the well-publicized failure of the anchovy catch off the coast of Peru. The reduction of the anchovy supply put pressure on soybeans, which are also an important animal feed. The going price of a bushel of soybeans in the United States rose from less than $3 in late 1971 to a peak of $12.27 in June 1973.

The weather was also a problem in 1972–73. There was a below-normal monsoon that cut India's grain crop in 1972. . . . [In 1973] floods wiped out harvests in Pakistan. And south of the Sahara, the countries in what is known as the Sahelian Belt—Mauritania, Mali, Chad, Senegal, Upper Volta, and Niger—suffered their sixth consecutive year of drought, which has severely affected both cattle and crops. [See articles on the Sahel in Section II, below.]

All these events contributed to higher food prices by reducing supply. In addition, prices were bolstered by the great worldwide economic boom, which steadily drove up demand. Meanwhile, the two devaluations of the dollar . . . made US food abnormally cheap abroad, and Japan, among other nations, loaded up on US supplies. . . .

Bad Luck With the Russians

The United States also had some bad luck—and some bad management—in its dealings with the Soviet Union, which needed grain after the 1972 harvest came up short. The bad luck began, in a sense, with a shift in Soviet policy. When the USSR has had poor crops in the past, it has liquidated part of its livestock herds, i.e., by feeding more meat to its citizens, it lessened the demand for grains. One trouble with this policy is that it takes years to rebuild depleted livestock herds; if the herds had been slaughtered in 1972, Soviet citizens would have had much less meat for a long time. Nowadays, however, there are intense new demands for higher standards of living in the Soviet Union, and there have been riots at food stores that run short of supplies.

In consequence, the government decided not to cut back when the 1972 grain harvest turned out to be a disaster (the official figures show a harvest of 168 million metric tons,

versus 181 million a year earlier). Instead, Soviet buyers
went into the world market to get wheat for their people
and feed grains for the livestock. Demand from the Soviet
Union accounted for a great deal of the additional grain
and feed exports that hit world markets beginning in 1972.

US agricultural officials did not spot this basic shift in
policy very early. One reason they did not is that the Soviet
buyers entered the US market very adroitly—for instance,
by first expressing a great interest in US corn and soybeans
when it was wheat that was really critical to them. As a
result of this shortage, the Russians were able to pick up
amazingly large quantities of grain at amazingly low
prices. . . .

And yet, for all the special circumstances of 1972–73,
there are reasons to wonder whether the pressure for higher
food prices might not emerge again—and on a permanent
basis. It is certain that world demand for food is on a long-
term uptrend. It is going to keep rising if only because
world population is likely to grow about 2.1 percent annually—a rate that represents about 75 million people a
year just now. The overall growth involves a 1.1 percent
annual increase in the developed countries and 2.4 percent
in the less developed world.

Furthermore, demand will grow more rapidly than population as people try to improve their diets. The FAO
projects that demand will increase 1.1 percent a year faster
than population in the developed countries and about 0.6
percent faster in the less developed ones.

The improvement in eating standards will be reflected
powerfully in two ways. In the poorer nations the principal
improvements are expected to come from adding new varieties or improved strains of cereals. In addition, people are
expected to get more proteins from vegetables, including
soybeans.

In the more developed countries, the improvements will
involve more meat, particularly beef. US consumption of

meat, mainly beef, pork, poultry, and fish, is already running about 250 pounds per capita. . . .

The Limits to Meat Eating

While demand for meat will surely be rising, it is also possible to discern some trends that may ease the pressure. One important trend has to do with the expanding use of soybeans to supply proteins. Soybeans, which have long been used to feed animals, are increasingly entering the human diet directly. In the United States, soybean products are now used in many baked foods, dessert toppings, Metrecal, and other prepared foods. There is also greater interest in the use of soybeans as meat extenders. They are used in, for example, canned chili con carne and meatballs and spaghetti. And . . . [in 1973] when meat prices began to soar, soybean preparations got their first big trial as additives to hamburger meat sold at meat counters. . . .

Next year the world will have 75 million more people to feed. Meanwhile, the overall pressure of demand on food supplies would be eased by anything—including higher meat prices—that led consumers to shift from meat to cereal products. Eating meat is a very inefficient way to consume grain; so is eating dairy products and eggs. It is estimated that cattle have to take in about seven pounds of grain in order to put on one pound themselves. The ratio for hogs is about four to one, for poultry about three to one. The average American consumes about 1,600 pounds of grain a year, but he eats only 150 of those pounds in the form of bread, cereals, cake, and the like. He takes in the balance indirectly, by eating a lot of meat. (A consumer in a less developed country puts away perhaps 400 pounds of grain, most of it eaten directly.)

For all the imponderables that affect the future demand for food, supply is a good deal more difficult to gauge. It can be affected, not only by economic considerations, but by changes in climate, in ecological conditions, and in several different technologies associated with food production.

The supply of beef, for example, would be enhanced considerably if other countries followed the lead of the United States and increased the proportion of animals brought to maturity on feedlots rather than on grazing lands; feedlot operations can speed up the growing process considerably. . . . It would also be much more economic for Europeans to eat more beef and less veal—because the weight of the animals being slaughtered would be greater. Then there is the possibility of getting cows to give birth to more than one calf at a time. Several different research approaches are now being explored in efforts to discover a "twinning" process that will produce a litter of two calves.

Yet most of the major opportunities for expanding the supply of meat abroad present problems. Raising more cattle would create a need for a major expansion of grazing lands, and some of that land would have to be irrigated to make it usable. Large-scale feedlot operations would create air- and water-pollution problems for nearby towns. And, of course, feeding all those additional animals would put still more pressures on the supplies of soybeans and feed grains.

What about the possibility of expanding soybean supplies? It seems likely that much of the additions to world soybean output will have to come in the United States—but several problems are involved in increasing United States output. One is that any rise in our total, which is around 1.5 million bushels now, will depend mainly on increases in acreage. In the past, farmers have found more acres for soybeans by shifting out of hay or small grains. But any sizable gains in the future will probably involve diverting acreage from corn. And the trouble with that is that soybean yields are smaller than corn yields per acre and increase much more slowly. Consequently, farmers would have to see a lot more profit in soybeans than in corn. Agricultural economists calculate that in the United States it takes a soybean price that is three times as high as that of corn to provide the incentive to divert acreage. . . .

Some Problems Down on the Farm

In many ways, American farmers have the problems of American businessmen: there is a powerful demand for their output but they are short of capacity; they have heavy debt charges, have trouble getting raw materials—and now confront a new range of uncertainties and cost pressures related to energy. The principal raw-material problem these days has to do with fertilizers. Several years ago, world capacity was greatly overbuilt, and many fertilizer plants were taken out of production. Today, there is a fertilizer squeeze, and there may be less available than will be needed for US plantings next spring. Potash is the only major kind of fertilizer in sufficient supply. Demand for phosphates is running ahead of production, while anhydrous ammonia is particularly scarce because its manufacture requires a lot of natural gas, which is itself scarce at the moment. US fertilizer prices had to be decontrolled . . . [in 1973] because so much of the available supply was being shipped abroad, where prices were well above the domestic ceilings. Domestic prices have since risen as much as 50 percent. [See "Fertilizer—Shortage and Supply," in this section, below.]

The long-run prospects for abatement of food price pressures are somewhat different from those in the short run. In the short run, we should get some abatement because harvests are generally expected to be abundant both here and abroad. . . . It is true that the Russians and others are still buying our grains and also true that worldwide grain stocks are low. Still, if the harvests turn out as expected, the price pressure will be less.

But prospects further out are not so favorable. It seems certain that demand for food will continue to rise—and uncertain that supplies can keep pace. On balance, the demand-and-supply relationship makes it likely that the price of food will go up—perhaps substantially. In addition, food producers face higher costs from a number of different directions, e.g., the costs involved in giving up some efficient pesticides that create ecological damage, and these may also boost prices.

The Bin May Be Empty

Meanwhile, it seems likely that food prices will fluctuate more from one year to another than they have in the past. . . . The world can no longer expect the US government to buy and accumulate excess stocks when prices fall below specific levels. Instead, US farmers will be selling their output of wheat and corn in a free market (they will be reimbursed to the extent that market prices fall below minimums announced by the government). Thus the US government, which has served for years as the world's principal storage bin, may no longer have immense backlogs of grain for the world to fall back on in emergencies.

FERTILIZER—SHORTAGE AND SUPPLY [4]

At the front of any discussion about world food problems today is the latest news about fertilizers. Many nations have based their food production goals on the assumption that fertilizers will be available in almost unlimited supply and at reasonable prices. But now there is panic because fertilizers are scarce and prices have skyrocketed. A common prediction is that massive famines are inevitable because we are running out of fertilizers.

For the next three to four years, there is reason for concern. The situation will be especially serious for countries relying heavily on fertilizer imports. In many cases, these are the same countries with the most critical food problems.

In the developing countries it is estimated that if the amount of fertilizer available fell short by 20 percent, grain production in these countries would be reduced about 5 percent. And this does not take into account potential

[4] From "The Fertilizer 'Panic,' " by D. L. McCune, director, International Fertilizer Development Staff, Tennessee Valley Authority. *War on Hunger.* 8:5-8. Je. '74.

drought on a localized basis, and other adverse weather conditions.

The short run outlook indeed is serious.

In the longer run, however, *the world need not starve due to a lack of fertilizers.* Known raw materials are adequate and technology exists to produce whatever fertilizer is needed. True, future prices will be higher than was common in the late 1960s and early 1970s, but they should ease somewhat as fertilizer supplies increase.

Reasons for Gloom

Certainly, there are plenty of statistics to justify concern. According to TVA estimates, world fertilizer consumption will reach 113 million metric tons by 1979/80, up from about 77.5 million tons in 1972/73. Average annual rates of increase will range from 8 to 11 percent in developing countries and from 4 to 8 percent in the developed countries. Although developing regions are expected to increase fertilizer use at a higher rate than the developed world, they will account for only one fourth of total use by 1980. Actual increases in the developed world between 1972/73 and 1979/80 are expected to be 27 million metric tons and 10 million metric tons in lesser developed countries, where increased food production is vital.

In terms of specific plant nutrients, world nitrogen use will increase from about 36 million metric tons in 1972/73 to 57 million metric tons in 1979/80. The developing world (including developing Asia) is expected to use 18 million metric tons of nitrogen or 32 percent of the total. Phosphate use is expected to rise from about 23 million metric tons in 1972/73 to 31 million metric tons by 1979/80. Only 7.4 million metric tons or 24 percent of the total will be used in the lesser developed countries by 1980. Potash use now stands at 19.4 million metric tons and will reach 25.6 million metric tons by 1979/80. The developing countries are expected to use only 14 percent of this 1980 total.

These requirements leave little room for rationalization.

Resources must be developed and made increasingly available.

The nitrogen supply is unlimited because its source is the air we breathe. Seventy-eight percent of the air is nitrogen. Since the principal building block for nitrogen fertilizers is ammonia (NH_3), a source of hydrogen is the critical factor. Even with escalating prices, hydrocarbons based on natural gas or petroleum derivatives remain the only economical source of hydrogen based on present technology. Other potential sources, but still much more expensive, are coal or water.

There must be more nitrogen production to meet the need for nitrogen. The United States, Japan, and Western Europe have been the primary producers of nitrogen fertilizer and have dominated the world nitrogen trade. But since these are the areas where the energy crisis is most critical, they are becoming less dependable sources for developing nations. Oil and gas-rich areas—such as the Persian Gulf, North Africa, USSR, Indonesia, Bangladesh, Nigeria, Venezuela, Ecuador, and Canada—must now produce nitrogen for countries with limited natural gas or petroleum.

World phosphate trade (rock phosphate or finished phosphatic fertilizers), has relied heavily upon Morocco and the United States. Both have the potential for expansion. Price of phosphate rock in the past six months has tripled from Morocco and doubled from the United States. Other potential producers and exporters, such as Australia, Peru, Angola, Spanish Sahara, and Jordan, need to be encouraged to meet increasing demand to provide alternate sources and reduce shipping distances.

Sulfur, one of the most plentiful elements in nature, is also essential for phosphatic fertilizer production. It is mined as elemental sulfur and as sulfur-containing minerals. Also, byproduct sulfur from smelting operations and sulfur extracted from natural gas and petroleum products are becoming increasingly important sources for fertilizer manufacture.

Potash production has been dominated by North America, Western Europe, and Eastern Europe. Although deposits in Canada and Eastern Europe can be expanded, new production points are needed to provide alternate sources and improved logistics to market. Potential producers appear to be Peru, Brazil, Thailand, and Ethiopia. There are expansion possibilities in the Congo. . . .

Cause for Optimism

It is easy to overlook favorable signs during times of stress and uncertainty. But they are there. Traditionally, the fertilizer industry is a responsive industry, but there is danger of overreaction leading to overproduction. Such overreaction in the late 1960s to the threat of famine in the mid-1960s is a major reason for the present shortages. Overbuilding of capacity for mining and production of fertilizers in the late 1960s caused prices to tumble. Older plants were closed and many dismantled and new plants were built at too slow a rate. This coupled with poor records on startup and poor production from plants in many developing countries permitted demand to catch up with production. Poor crop years in 1971 and 1972 with high prices for grains and other farm products unexpectedly increased fertilizer demand faster than the industry could satisfy it.

Fertilizer prices are now at an all time high and the industry is responding. *It appears that adequate capacity is being built to meet anticipated long-range needs.* In fact, caution may be needed to prevent the pendulum from swinging so far that production will again greatly exceed demand.

Need for Some Insurance

Increasingly, there seems to be a need for some insurance to help guarantee adequate food supplies. There is talk of the need for a world food bank. Others propose a world fertilizer bank. Both are noble gestures but fraught with problems. Another possible solution—and one that might be more workable—would be to bank fertilizer production capacity. During periods of oversupply, strategically located plants could be retired from production and placed in "mothballs" until the pendulum again swings the other way. This was done in effect in Canada when Saskatchewan limited potash production. It also is done by individual companies when they shut down their less efficient plants in times of surplus supply and low prices, then reopen them when the profitability has improved.

Surely we can anticipate by six months or a year when food supplies will be critically short. Standby plants can then quickly be brought back on-stream.

The same concept could extend to the basic resources part of the industry to keep it alive and productive. For example, phosphate and potash mines could continue to operate with the raw materials being shipped to and stored at key manufacturing locations throughout the world. Both phosphate and sulfur can easily be stockpiled.

To make such a bank work, some international body or the major countries must be willing to organize such a system. It probably would be no more costly or certainly less unwieldy than a world food bank, a world fertilizer bank or subsidizing farmers to not produce certain food and fiber crops.

Any such plan could successfully keep the fertilizer industry intact at all times, more closely match the supply with the demand, promote greater efficiency within the industry with resulting savings to the consumer, and help prevent world food levels from sinking to dangerously low levels.

THE CRISIS IN PERSPECTIVE [5]

"There has never been a time in the recorded history of the world when all people have had enough food to pre-

[5] From an address by William A. Hewitt, chairman, Deere & Company, delivered at Dartmouth College, February 18, 1975. Dartmouth College. Department of Geography. Hanover, N.H., 03755. '75. Mimeo. Reprinted by permission.

vent malnutrition or, at times, actual famine and starvation. But available evidence indicates that the world has come closer to that goal during the past quarter-century than at any time in the past three hundred years." These are not my words; they are from a recent statement by Dr. D. Gale Johnson, Chairman of the University of Chicago's Department of Economics and one of the world's leading analysts of agricultural economics. At a time when the general mood of many people concerning the ability of our planet to survive is decidedly pessimistic, Dr. Johnson's statement strikes an essential note of realism and perspective.

What are the circumstances, historical and otherwise, that we need to be aware of as we discuss this problem? For one thing, the problem of hunger is not new. During recent history, recurring fears of world starvation have appeared at intervals. . . . Nor is the problem of hunger currently worse than it has been. According to Professor Johnson, there have been fewer famines in the last quarter-century than in any other during the past three hundred years. And the number of famine deaths during the past twenty-five years has been but a small fraction of the well-documented deaths during the last quarter of the nineteenth century. . . .

Not only has the bulk of humanity been eating more; it has also been eating better. One important indication of improving nutrition is a longer life span. A child born in one of the developing countries in 1950 could expect to live to age thirty-five or forty. A child born there today can expect to live to fifty-two. Though this statistic is still far short of the average for children born in affluent countries, it represents genuine progress in both the fields of nutrition and health care. Essentially the overall food situation in the world has been improving for two decades.

Because of what we see in newspapers, magazines, and on television, there is a terrifying irony in that last statement. The reason for it is that our perception of the problem of food shortages has changed. Today, in an age of virtually instant communications, what was previously out of sight, out of mind, for most well-fed people is now brought quickly and dramatically before us. Our level of consciousness has been raised. In the privacy of our homes, thousands of miles from the actual scene, we can witness starvation on the streets of Calcutta almost as it occurs. Or, for a view of the effects of malnutrition, we can switch channels and see a line-up of those afflicted by kwashiorkor in parts of Africa. . . . [Kwashiorkor is a severe disease of young children caused by chronic malnutrition.—Ed.]

Warnings of a fast-approaching doomsday appear vividly before us in the pages of magazines and books, as well as on television and in newspapers. Some are replete with charts proving beyond doubt that the inviolable laws of exponential growth decree a coming world of undernourished, wall-to-wall people.

The tendency of some of us, I think, is to conclude that little can be done. Pessimism bears down on us. Some among us even begin seriously to think of triage: the ghastly life-boat ethic which holds that hopelessly food-short peoples must be abandoned to the ravages of famine for the benefit of those for whom there exists some hope of being saved. [See "Living on a Lifeboat," in Section IV, below.] In these circumstances, it is imperative to apply an historical sense and a careful analysis to the bewildering volume of information that inundates us, and not succumb to the paralysis of pessimism. We need to understand that whatever we do probably will not succeed perfectly. But our attempts at solutions will have a greater chance of success if they are founded on a realistic, concerned but nonsensational, analysis of the problem. . . .

We need to remember, too, that the term "developing countries" obscures the great diversity among the nations of the world and leaves the impression that there are only two kinds—the wealthy and well-fed like the United States, and the poor and food-short like Bangladesh. Yet surely there is a difference between the food problems of a developing nation like oil-abundant Saudi Arabia and a developing nation like desperately poor Ethiopia. As regards food production, many developing countries are, in fact, largely self-sufficient even though their industry, their educational system, what in general might be called their infrastructure, are by our terms backward and inadequate.

The United Nations has published a list of the forty poorest countries. On it are Kenya, Burma, the Malagasy Republic, Cambodia and Malawi. Yet all of these are normally net exporters of food grains. Even Niger, one of the six West African countries hardest hit recently by drought and famine, is in normal times a net exporter of food grains. . . .

There are those who observe, and properly so, that the potential for growing more food worldwide is impressive. Vast tracts of land can be brought into production in the Amazon basin, but not until we can learn how to farm productively in tropical rain forest soils. Millions of acres in Africa can supply food if the tsetse fly, carrier of sleeping sickness, can be controlled. The use of tillage practices, irrigation methods, and disease-resistant crop strains that are already known can ameliorate food production problems in many lands. And there are the laboratory possibilities: better protein content in cereal grains, animal feed from algae, protein from petroleum, hybridization of additional species of plants and animals. But all these elements represent promise, not current reality. They cannot yet be regarded as a panacea for the world's food problems, lacking only application of the necessary will. The reality is that the great majority of crops to meet the demands of a growing world for more and better food currently come from, and in all likelihood will continue to come from, farmlands between the thirtieth and fifty-fifth parallels of north latitude. And, to a lesser extent, from farmlands between the same parallels of south latitude.

By and large, although important agricultural areas exist in other latitudes, the temperate zones offer the world's most advanced and most productive farming. They comprise its chief green belts. They produce the bulk of the essential food and fiber the world depends upon. The agricultural industry has been stressing the importance of these two green belts for almost a decade. In that time, no scientific or other advances have occurred to diminish or change the importance of the temperate zones. In the northern hemisphere, the principal green belt areas include most of the United States, southern Canada, Europe, the northern edge of Africa, parts of Soviet Asia, and mainland China. Some of these areas—Soviet Asia, parts of western states like Nevada and Utah—lack adequate rainfall or have other defects that restrict their agricultural productivity. Below the equator, the 30° to 55° green belt is primarily ocean. The most significant agricultural areas in this green belt of the Southern Hemisphere are Argentina, the southern tip of Africa, and southern Australia.

As we add up all of the highly arable land in the areas I have identified, we see that the world must depend for the major portion of its agricultural production on only about 4 percent of the earth's land area. When one examines that 4 percent in detail, the extraordinary importance of the United States as a food supplier becomes apparent. Few, if any, other areas have as favorable a climate and such a vast and fertile land mass, so educated a farm population, so advanced an agricultural technology, so complete a storehouse of agricultural information, or so capable a corps of agricultural researchers. The result is that a considerable part of the world already depends upon the United States for food. We are the world's largest supplier of food by far.

THE CRISIS CONTINUES [6]

The world food crisis has not gone away.
Although the incipient famines of last summer and fall

[6] From "Food Experts See Several Countries in Greater Peril of Hunger and Possible Starvation Than Last Year," by Boyce Rensberger, staff writer. New York Times. p 34. Je. 3, '75. © 1975 by the New York Times Company. Reprinted by permission.

were relieved through a variety of short-term measures and public attention to the topic has faded in recent months, some agricultural experts say a number of countries may now be in greater peril of hunger, malnutrition and possible starvation than they were a year ago.

Although no major crop failures have been reported or forecast this year, the experts are fearful because the world's margin of food reserves has narrowed considerably over the last year.

They are also worried that the currently optimistic crop forecasts are fostering a sense of complacency that could lead to a slackening of long-range efforts to establish a global food reserve system and to improve agriculture in the poor countries.

The world's supply of reserve grain, which was already precariously low early last summer [1974] is even smaller now. Much of it was used for famine relief last year and global crop shortfalls of about 66 million tons last year prevented any significant rebuilding of stocks.

Population Has Risen

In the year since the early signs of last year's food shortages began to appear, the world's population has grown by about 74 million mouths. . . .

According to a confidential evaluation of the food supply situation around the world, shortages now exist in Bangladesh, Yemen, Somalia, Tanzania, Rwanda, Burundi, Malawi and Mozambique and there is a danger of food shortage in Sri Lanka.

Earlier . . . [in 1975] Kenya was listed as suffering a food shortage but the situation there is said to have improved.

Thus, a modest spell of bad weather that would have had little impact in past years could now precipitate a sizeable food shortage. If, as some climatologists suspect, the world is experiencing a major shift in weather patterns, . . . [1974's] disastrous weather could be repeated this summer.

So far, however, the early Food and Agriculture Organization [FAO] forecasts are that this year's global harvest will be 8 percent above last year's. Since 1974 was a poor year, most of the predicted improvement represents only a return to normal.

According to the FAO estimates, most of that increase will come from the United States and the Soviet Union while expectations are for declines in the crops of Western Europe, North Africa and the Near East. India's winter wheat crop, now being harvested, is expected to set a record high. The failure of this crop last year was a major factor in India's famine.

A Crucial Year

Over all, the FAO in its May 16 [1975] quarterly report, "Food Outlook," said, "The food situation has improved in the last quarter, but the world still depends crucially on this year's crop outturn. Early prospects are favorable for wheat and coarse grains, but weather could still play havoc with spring-sown crops. The outlook is uncertain for rice."

The FAO projections, which largely agree with those of the United States Department of Agriculture, are based on the assumption that weather for the rest of the growing season will be favorable in all major agricultural regions of the world.

That is the same assumption that was made last spring when the forecasts were also for good harvests. As it turned out, bad weather, chiefly drought, afflicted significant portions of North America, the Soviet Union and India.

Most observers credit last year's poor harvests and the World Food Conference in Rome with stimulating a new and needed interest in agricultural development. [See "The Eradication of Hunger," in Section VI, below.]

Experts Are Worried

Even if this year's forecasts turn out to be accurate and harvests are good, many agricultural experts are worried because they say that one good crop year could erode the new sense of urgency about the need for long-range measures to improve food production in the food-deficit countries. They fear that a season of good crops could also sap momentum that has begun to build toward establishing an international system of grain reserves for famine prevention.

Most food experts agree that, even in the absence of outbreaks of hunger because of fluctuating weather, it will be impossible to meet the growing demand for food without strong political commitments to agriculture at the national level in the developing countries.

So long as these countries could turn to the United States and purchase cheap "surplus" food or receive it as direct aid, their domestic crop failures had little impact. Now that the United States and other major exporters are no longer able to supply much cheap food or free food, the food-deficit countries are said to be coming to recognize the need to upgrade their own farming methods.

"Despite all the nice, optimistic projections on crops, some of those crops haven't even been planted yet," said Dr. Dale Hathaway, an agricultural economist at the Ford Foundation. . . . "We're right back where we were in 1974 at about this time except that stocks are lower than ever."

Dr. Hathaway noted that to cope with last year's food shortages the Indian government was forced to purchase about 7 million tons of grain at commercial rates. This used up a large portion of India's foreign exchange and has set back the country's development plans.

Should another major food shortage develop, Dr. Hathaway said India would be less able to cope with it than before. . . .

James P. Grant, president of the [Overseas Development Council, a private organization], agrees with many other observers that the key to stabilizing food supply and prices is to establish a world food reserve system that can buy up grain in a good year (keeping the price from falling too far) and release it in a poor year (to rescue the hungry and keep prices from rising too far).

"In the absence of a system of reserves," Mr. Grant said, "the world food situation continues to be very precarious and probably will remain that way for some time."

Since the Rome food conference, few firm steps have been taken toward setting up a food reserve and many observers say that the chief stumbling block has been the reluctance of the United States, by far the world's leading producer of exportable grain, to assume a major share of the burden or to exercise any leadership toward creating such a system.

Many food experts say it would be a great tragedy if the optimistic crop forecasts were borne out with bumper crops and there were no food reserve system to acquire some of the excess production.

II. FAMINE

EDITOR'S INTRODUCTION

From biblical times, the world has known the dread Four Horsemen of the Apocalypse: war, famine, pestilence, and death. Considering our state of scientific advancement, it is ironic that famine is with us yet in the twentieth century world.

This section examines the face of famine in the world today, beginning with stark statistics from *U.S. News & World Report.* The following selection is a general review by John H. Douglas of the causes and forewarnings of famine and an exploration of possible solutions. Vincent S. Kearney, senior associate editor of *America,* and Alan Matt Warhaftig describe the most critical famine region in today's world—the Sahel, in Central Africa. Jean Mayer, noted professor of nutrition and authority on world food problems, reviews other famine areas of the past decade.

WHERE 700 MILLION PEOPLE FACE STARVATION [1]

Reprinted from *U.S. News & World Report.*

United Nations food experts say that thirty-two countries around the globe are desperately short of food. These nations are hard pressed to buy the grain, fertilizer and petroleum needed to stave off starvation for 700 million of their total populations of 900 million. The thirty-two countries, and their populations—

India	574,200,000
Bangladesh	71,600,000
Pakistan	66,800,000
Ethiopia	26,100,000
Sudan	16,900,000

[1] Chart from "As Famine Spreads—What's to Be Done." *U.S. News & World Report.* 77:87. N. 18, '74.

Tanzania	14,400,000
Sri Lanka	13,300,000
Kenya	12,500,000
Ghana	9,400,000
Madagascar	8,000,000
Cambodia	7,600,000
Cameroon	6,200,000
Yemen Arab Republic	6,100,000
Upper Volta	5,700,000
Mali	5,400,000
Haiti	5,200,000
Ivory Coast	4,600,000
Niger	4,300,000
Guinea	4,200,000
Senegal	4,200,000
Chad	3,900,000
El Salvador	3,900,000
Laos	3,200,000
Somalia	3,000,000
Dahomey	2,900,000
Sierra Leone	2,900,000
Honduras	2,800,000
Central African Republic	1,700,000
Democratic Republic of Yemen	1,600,000
Mauritania	1,300,000
Lesotho	1,000,000
Guyana	800,000

FACING THE THREAT [2]

Omens of Famine

Like cancer, starvation seldom kills its victims directly. Rather, it weakens the whole fabric of life until the frailest

[2] From "The Omens of Famine" and "Confronting Famine," by John H. Douglas, science and society editor. Science News. 105:306-8, 322-3. My. 11-18, '74. Reprinted with permission from Science News, the weekly news magazine of science and the applications of science, copyright 1974 by Science Service, Inc.

part gives, then the rest disintegrates. For an individual, the end usually comes by disease; for a society, by anarchy. Famine, like cancer, is easiest stopped before it spreads, and now danger signals from many areas of the world have become unmistakable. . . .

  / The inherent fragility [of economic development] is what a walk down any thoroughfare in Asia . . . [reveals]: A few rich living among many poor, the two thirds of the world's population that must scrap for a quarter of its protein; a few tractors, which, without fuel, cannot harvest the green revolution crops that depend on them; most important, only a few domestic sources of fertilizer, a petroleum product without which the new, productive grain hybrids cannot grow.

Development has brought dependence. Machinery, petroleum and fertilizer are, for most developing countries, import items. The economies of many small countries are narrowly based on some abundant local commodity, such as rubber or gold, and when population pressures outstrip the land's capacity for growing crops, limited foreign exchange capability must be used to buy food. Whereas before World War II Western Europe was the only grain deficit region on earth, now only North America and Australia remain as net grain exporters. The United States and Canada together have a greater stranglehold on the world's food exports than the Arabs have on petroleum. . . .

The world's poor must compete with the rising affluence of the world's rich. Food consumption does not increase linearly with wealth. On the contrary, as income rises, people eat less grain directly and begin to eat more meat, which requires as much as seven times the grain, as feed, to put an equivalent amount of protein on the table. Just at a time when the United States faced a humiliating dollar devaluation and rising balance of payments deficit, agricultural exports suddenly doubled, becoming the most important single item in the country's international trade picture. A bad harvest in Siberia led to the largest single agricultural sale in history, depleting the remaining US stored grain reserves. Suddenly surpluses became too valuable to give away.

With malevolent coincidence, the world's climate almost simultaneously began to change. . . . The desert-creating high-pressure areas that lie between the monsoon rains to the south and the cold circumpolar winds to the north began to migrate toward the equator, bringing drought to regions of Africa, China, South Asia, India and Central America. Climatology is a young and inexact science, but the few specialists willing to speak up on the subject say the recent changes are the apparent result of a global cooling trend that has lowered the earth's temperature 2.7 degrees F. since 1945. The best evidence from ice and sediment records indicates that weather over the last half century has been the warmest in 1,000 years and that a cycle of colder temperatures can be expected. The effect would be a major shift of rain patterns and deserts, and a shorter growing season for northern latitudes.

The sub-Sahara row of six countries, known collectively as the Sahel region, presents a grim test case of what may happen in more populous areas if droughts spread. . . .

The Indian subcontinent may be next, according to Lester R. Brown, a senior fellow at the Overseas Development Council in Washington and an outspoken observer in matters of world food supplies. Even before the energy crisis hit, the world appeared to be at the "bust end of a cycle" in world fertilizer industry. . . . [See "An Emerging Chronic Global Scarcity," in Section I, above.]

India appears most vulnerable. Even India's own National Council of Applied Economic Research admits: "Sometimes the very immensity of the problem numbs one's senses and impairs the capacity to deal with it." . . . Riots have already occurred in two states. Kerosene for cooking has risen beyond the price reach of many. Inflation gallops along at 25 percent a year, and half of India's total export earnings may have to go to buy oil. . . .

China would be better off, except for the fertilizer problem. That country has, in many ways, worked an economic miracle, almost abolishing malnutrition without substantially raising per capita income. But much of China's foreign exchange goes for fertilizer; it is the world's largest importer, buying mostly from Japan, which has now been severely hit by the energy crisis. China is also the current number one US wheat customer, even in good weather. With an intricate irrigation system, China is better prepared to meet drought than India, but should fertilizer continue scarce, China too could face severe difficulty.

No one knows when the crunch will come, but Lester Brown says that within a year, leaders of the world's developed countries may be faced with the agonizing decision of whether to "cut Asia adrift" or ration food at home to feed starving millions abroad.

On any street in Asia one can smell the pungent aroma of the local, highly spiced cuisine. How hard to believe that too is so terribly fragile.

Confronting Famine

The world is about as ready to face a major famine now as when the biblical Joseph warned Pharaoh to save grain for seven lean years ahead.

Global food reserves have hit their lowest level in two decades, though the number of hungry mouths has grown by half in that time. Spreading droughts and the energy crisis have conspired to negate the food production advances of the green revolution. New scientific and technological advances offer much promise of helping feed the world over the long run; but for the time being, only the closest sort of international cooperation and genuine philanthropy on the part of industrialized nations can possibly rebuild reserves enough to buffer shortages that are likely to develop throughout the Third World in the next couple of years. Judging from citizen reactions to other shortages, these are poor times to implore new sacrifices.

American agricultural wealth still holds the key. Out of

some 1.2 billion tons of grain produced each year in the world (1972 figures), only about 90 million tons is free to move in international trade. Of that, 70 million tons comes from the United States. In the past, poorer nations have been able to draw upon American food resources in time of need; but rising affluence in Russia, Western Europe and Japan has steadily eroded this country's reserves of stored grain and now has boosted prices for new harvest surpluses above what developing nations can afford to pay. The energy crisis was the final straw. Faced with a balance-of-payments crisis over imported oil, America has pulled out all the stops—returning soil-bank land to active use, depleting reserves, removing planting restrictions—to increase production of the nation's most lucrative export item, food. . . .

Geographic concentration of excess grain production in the midwest regions of Canada and the United States holds another potential threat for Third World nutritional security. These "breadbasket" regions undergo regular cycles of drought—not related to the apparent overall change of global climate—and the next drought period, which might last five or six years, is due just about now. The last such period, during the fifties, wasn't so bad, but the one before that changed the region into the "Dust Bowl." Even a mild failure of the US grain crop could spell disaster for millions of people on the other side of the globe.

Even if adequate international food reserves could be set up, however, evidence from the current famine regions of Africa suggests the present system of delivering emergency food aid is clumsy, at best, and that much more sophisticated understanding of basic human needs during a crisis is also required.

Too often, donating countries do not take into account local diet and tolerances when they send relief packages of food. Favorite items include cans of sweetened, condensed milk and mounds of powdered, skimmed milk. While such provisions might be appropriate for disaster relief involving Caucasians of Northern European descent, the majority of the world's people develop, early in life, an intolerance to the principal sugar in cow's milk, lactose. Not only does it do them no good, it can produce dehydration and diarrhea —the last thing one wants to happen to a person suffering from starvation. In many cultures, the only milk product consumed by adults is yogurt, which has a lower level of lactose, and to send massive shipments of whole milk to a famine-stricken people without first testing for lactose intolerance is a classic example of what one food expert calls "ethnic chauvinism."

As with so many other complex problems, early warning of famine is crucial, but governments are often reticent to admit the need for emergency provisions until a crisis can no longer be hidden. In Ethiopia, for example, where 90 percent of the 25 million inhabitants live by subsistence farming, rainfall and harvests have been failing for eight years. The first government call for help did not come until April 1973, with the start of international emergency aid delayed until October. By the beginning of . . . [1974] relief teams from half a dozen nations were working in refugee camps, but these serve only an estimated 1 percent of the affected population. Meanwhile, in stricken rural areas, stock losses are estimated at 80 percent, and human deaths have been variously counted at 50,000 to 100,000. . . .

The issue is finally a moral one: Will the United States and other industrialized countries be willing to cut back on meat consumption to free grain for the world's poor? Famines in some areas, like the Sahel, have little direct effect on daily American life; but one in India would surely lead to some sort of armed confrontation, into which the United States seems always to be drawn. New Arab wealth must also be considered, for a rising standard of living in the Middle East will exert additional pressure on prices of food, particularly rice.

Already the national secretary of the National Farmers Union has told a Senate subcommittee, "Many farmers view permanent scarcity of food as a goal that would be appropriate to their self interest." We may soon find out whether this is also the attitude of the American people as a whole. Will the citizens of the Middle East and of the Western industrial countries accept the necessary sacrifices when they come, or will they, as C. P. Snow predicted long ago, sit and watch on the evening news millions of people dying of starvation, somewhere else? [See "The Most Important Questions," in Section IV, below.]

TRAGEDY IN THE SAHEL [3]

The now tragic effects of the years of drought in West Africa have nowhere been more graphically described than in Geoffrey Moorhouse's recently published *The Fearful Void*—an account of one man's abortive trek across the Sahara, a venture never before attempted by a lone European.

From Faguibine onwards [writes Moorhouse] the most recent effects of the long drought had been apparent—first a sheep with green guts coiled along its flank, later a donkey with its teeth drawn in a dying bray of abandoned hope. Here a cow and three goats were scattered across a few hundred square yards, puffed up with gases and stinking so horribly that ould Mohammed lit a Gauloise as he rode, and I wound my headcloth tightly round my nose.

Such livestock losses are being measured in the millions today in this region of Africa known as the Sahel [consisting of all or part of Mali, Niger, Chad, Upper Volta, Mauritania, and Senegal], where an entire nomadic way of life is being threatened with extinction by one of the most devastating droughts in modern times. The catastrophe has dealt no less harshly with human beings. William Price, Britain's Overseas Development Minister, estimates the number of people facing starvation at 5 million. UN Secretary General Kurt Waldheim would double that figure. Whichever is cor-

[3] From "The Sahel: Tragedy of Underdevelopment," by Vincent S. Kearney, S.J., senior associate editor. *America*. 131:67-9. Ag. 24. '74. Reprinted with permission of *America*, 1974. All rights reserved. © 1974 by America Press, 106 W. 56th Street, New York, N.Y. 10019.

rect, hundreds of thousands have already died, and there is no respite in sight. If, as some climatologists fear, the crisis is but the initial stage of a thirty-year period of diminishing rainfall, a significant portion of the African continent is likely to be lost to the encroaching, arid sands of the Sahara.

Sahel is an Arabic word meaning shore. As a geographical designation, it refers to that region of Africa that touches on the southern extremity of the Sahara Desert, forming a belt that stretches clear across Africa for thousands of miles. Even in normal times it is an inhospitable area. It is the home of nomads, with their wandering herds of cattle, camels and ubiquitous goats, and of other sedentary peoples who are scattered about in thousands of villages, subsisting on millet and sorghum crops. . . . [In 1973] alone, the desert advanced sixty miles into the Sahel, covering village huts with sand and forcing a mass migration of people southward. The flight in search of water has caused considerable economic and social upheaval, whose consequences have not yet been reckoned with.

The region is the victim of one of nature's unpredictable quirks. The devastating drought is thought to be the result of a basic shift in weather patterns that is causing a progressive reduction in rainfall the Sahel can ill afford. Normal precipitation, which is confined to a July-August rainy season, is sparse enough. If the theory of permanent meteorological change is sound, there is little that human ingenuity can devise to check the inevitable onward march of the Sahara. Meanwhile, despite crash relief programs, the tragic human problem intensifies with each passing month.

According to the experts of the European Economic Community, . . . half the 12 million inhabitants of the Sahel are face to face with starvation. In Mauritania, pitiful harvests and the loss of 60 to 80 percent of the livestock have left three quarters of the population without adequate nourishment. In Senegal, almost a million people are without food. Mali's problems have intensified as the desert-dwelling Tuareg have made for the banks of the Niger. The tragedy of human suffering repeats itself in Upper Volta, Niger, Nigeria and Chad, and has moved beyond the Sahel proper into parts of the Sudan, into Ethiopia and even southward into Kenya.

The forced migrations of the nomadic populations and of the river-dwellers into the towns has had social repercussions that have begun to complicate the already baffling economic problems of these developing countries. . . .

This drought in the Sahel, of course, is not the first natural tragedy in human history. Somehow or other, man always manages to survive the vagaries of nature. And yet the Western world cannot view with complacency what is happening in this vast region of Africa. For it demonstrates how devastating the impact of a natural catastrophe can be to a people whose normal lives are lived on the thin edge between mere subsistence and starvation. This is one of the curses of the underdeveloped world. Its people find it infinitely more difficult to withstand the scourges of an errant, unpredictable nature. The fact that, for them, the problem is so often compounded by the incompetence of governments does not help.

It took the world at large a long time to react to this tragedy. Hesitant African governments must perhaps shoulder the major portion of the blame. The serious consequences of the drought were plainly foreseeable toward the end of 1972. In fact, French experts had raised warning signals in October of that year. As late as . . . May [1973], however, at the meeting of the Organization of African Unity (OAU) then being held in Addis Ababa, not a single African head of state so much as alluded to the famine seriously affecting close to a dozen states on the continent. To sound the alarm would have amounted to an implied admission of their lack of foresight. Besides, it would have laid open to the world the misery of their people and the embarrassing fragility of their economics.

Ironically, the tragedy was already playing itself out within a relatively few miles of the very conference hall in

Addis Ababa itself. Six months previously, the Ethiopian
Ministry of Agriculture had released a confidential report
warning of the failure of rainfall and crops and urging the
need for "major food imports" in 1973. An embarrassed
Ethiopian government swept the document under the rug.
It was not until three months later that its complacency was
shaken when bands of starving refugees from the stricken
provinces began arriving in Addis Ababa to confront government and tourists with the unmistakable evidence of
misery in the hinterlands. They were quickly turned back
by the police, and the government took wishful comfort in
the assurances of the governor of Wollo province that,
though there was a slight problem of drought, everything
was under control.

Meanwhile, the world had no intimation of the extent
of the famine in Ethiopia until the midsummer of 1973,
when an official of the UN International Children's Emergency Fund (UNICEF) made public in Addis Ababa a report that 60,000 people in Wollo province alone had died
of starvation. The refusal of the Ethiopian government to
face reality and the incompetence and corruption revealed
when it finally sought to come to grips with the problem
precipitated the political crisis in the country that apparently is yet to run its course.

But at least the news was out. Unfortunately, the initial
response of world governments to the crisis left as much to
be desired as the incompetence of the African governments
themselves. . . .

Nevertheless, the aid did begin to flow. The Sahel was
declared a disaster area by the heads of six African states
who met to form a committee that would devise ways to
cope with the problem of the drought. An appeal was made
to France (whose former colonial ties make the area of the
Sahel one of special French interest), which shipped 65,000
tons of foodstuffs. The European Economic Community
contributed 210,000 tons of cereals and 13,000 tons of powdered milk. The UN through such specialized agencies as

the UN Development Program, the Food and Agriculture
Organization (FAO) and UNICEF soon joined the relief
effort. [But] the crisis is far from over.

THE SAHEL FACES THE FUTURE [4]

Lord, Hearken to my voice, *Let It Rain.* It rains
And you have opened from your arms of thunder the
    cataracts of forgiveness.

The image created by Léopold Sédar Senghor in these
lines from "Elegy of the Waters" is elemental—close to the
earth and water cycle that sustains it. Water is the blood
of the earth; without water there can be no harvests, no
erosion (change), no life.

For seven long painful years there was a drought in
Senghor's native Senegal and other nations of the Sudano-
Sahel region of Africa. Whether by divine providence, as
suggested in Senghor's elegy or by meteorological chance,
[in 1975] the rains have returned to the Sahel, ending the
drought and bringing some relief to the atrophied land and
the people who live and work on it. Life can emerge again
in the Sahel, which for so long has only known the torturous
negation of life.

While many observations remain to be made about the
image created by Senghor—its style, context and assumptions
—the purpose of this essay is to pose several important questions about the drought and the famine which accompanied
it; and in so doing to suggest some issues which must be
confronted if future tragedies are to be prevented in the
Sahel.

From the outset, the distinction needs to be drawn between drought and famine, for they are not the same.
Drought is a natural phenomenon defined by a prolonged
absence of rainfall; famine is a social phenomenon charac-

[4] From "Famine in Africa: No Act of God," by Alan Matt Warhaftig, teaching
and research assistant, Stanford University. *Nation.* 220:197-200. F. 22, '75. Reprinted by permission.

terized by an acute shortage of food. Drought does not necessarily lead to famine, at least in the short run. It is unthinkable that drought in Scandinavia or some other economically developed region would cause famine. Agricultural production in such regions features highly developed technologies, including sophisticated irrigation systems which can transport water to areas deprived of it. That is not true of the Sahel. Also, an industrially developed nation confronted by drought can use the surplus created in non-agricultural sectors of its economy to trade with other nations for the food commodities it could not produce. But the nations of the Sahel are not industrially developed. . . .

The inability of the Sahelian states (Mali, Niger, Chad, Upper Volta, Mauritania and Senegal) to prevent famine during the recent drought cannot be understood apart from their historic experience of colonialism. While colonialism came to Africa later than to other parts of the world, its guiding principle, that colonies exist for the economic benefit of the colonizer, remained intact.

This principle, an extension of mercantilist economic doctrine, is evident in the Sahelian nations since colonization. The economies of the region, when they have developed at all, have done so with a greater emphasis on their roles as inputs to and markets for *métropolitain* French economy than as Sahelian economies designed to meet the economic needs of the people of the region.

Thus vertical economic linkages have been created—that is, links to the economy of the colonizing nation—rather than horizontal economic linkages which are those between the various sectors of the local economies. From this sort of development emerges the "mono-economy," the economy which produces little more than primary commodities: unprocessed mineral resources and agricultural goods which are exported for processing and consumption.

Statistics released by the Special Sahelian Office of the United Nations Secretariat support this characterization. The five Sahelian states other than Mauritania, whose iron ore accounts for 89.3 percent of its annual exports, export mostly unprocessed agricultural commodities such as cotton, groundnuts, oilseeds, fish and live animals, which account for 83 percent of their annual exports.

This type of development condemns these nations to a vicious circle of dependent-underdevelopment. As these countries are not economically self-sufficient, both because of their generally meager economic resources and the patterns of development mentioned above, they must trade with other nations for both consumer goods and the capital goods they require for economic development. The problem is that, because these economies produce mostly primary commodities which embody very little labor time relative to that embodied in processed consumer goods, little mobilizable capital is generated when these commodities are sold on the international market. Simply stated, these countries receive a low price for their exports relative to the prices they must pay for imports. Thus these countries lose out on both ends of exchange, a situation that supports the contention that dependent-underdevelopment is chronic and structural. . . .

The Sahel is severely underdeveloped. Statistics released by the UN show that 87 percent of the population of these countries is engaged in agricultural production. Considering this high proportion, the productivity of this sector is extremely low, averaging 43 percent of the gross domestic product of the six countries in 1969.

This low agricultural productivity is very much a legacy of colonialism. While the French found it in their interest to promote development in the mining sector of the Mauritanian economy and in the manufacturing sector of the Senegalese economy, they did not find it profitable to develop the agricultural sectors of either of these economies or those of the other Sahelian states.

Thus, the agricultural technologies employed in the Sahel are often centuries old. They are almost entirely labor-intensive and often, as in the case of slash and burn cultiva-

tion, harmful to the land. Irrigation systems are rare, so that
drought conditions pose a desperate threat. The result is
that agricultural yields are very low with respect both to
labor time and to the land area under cultivation.

The problems of agriculture are aggravated by the attention given to the cultivation of nonsubsistence crops—"cash
crops," as they are called. These, primarily cotton and
groundnuts, occupy nearly 20 percent of the areas under
cultivation and are grown for export rather than domestic
consumption. Again, with the exception of Mauritania,
these cash crops amount to nearly half of the annual exports of the Sahel.

While such crops were grown in the Sahel well before
the arrival of the French colonizers, it was the French who
stimulated their widespread cultivation by imposing taxes
on the population which had to be paid in francs. The only
way that a peasant could obtain francs was to cultivate
crops to be sold at markets where the franc was the currency
of exchange—i.e., markets that handled the "cash crops."
Therefore the energies and resources of the agricultural
population were diverted from their central responsibility
to produce enough food for the society to subsist. . . .

The people of the Sahel must consider carefully how
they are to apply the economic surplus created by their
labors. . . . While they've been told that the Western industrial model, with its centralization, urbanization and
capital-intensive technologies, is the only one for a modern
nation to follow, the people of the Sahel may well deem it
totally inappropriate to their needs. They may find that
cultivating nonsubsistence cash crops is not the best disposi-
tion of agricultural land or labor; that they would be better
advised to grow grains such as sorghum and millet which
could be converted to domestic consumption as well as exported.

One last consideration relates to the concept held by
these Sahelian countries of the sovereignty of the nation-
state and its relations with other nation-states. The present

division of states in the Sahel is arbitrary, the boundaries having been drawn for the convenience of colonial administration. Many of the Sahelian states have very little economic potential, given their meager mineral resources, hostile climates and geography (four of the six are landlocked). This leaves a nation such as Upper Volta in rather desperate circumstances, regardless of the decisions it makes concerning its future.

It seems fair to say that many of these nations cannot achieve development along the lines of any model without a closer cooperation with other dependent-underdeveloped nations in the region and around the world. If the industrialized nations cannot or will not help them, they must help one another to break the ensnarement of chronic dependence and underdevelopment and improve their lives collectively.

These points having been made, it must be said that decisions regarding the development and future of the Sahel must be made by the people of the region themselves, for they must live with their decisions or perhaps die in attempting to create a society they envision as their own. No solution can be imposed by international organizations or intellectuals from the industrialized nations, however well-intentioned they might be.

That does not relieve the industrialized countries of a moral responsibility to help the people of the Sahel; on the contrary, the industrialized nations should do all that they can. But it does emphasize that the Sahelian nations should not count on the help of the industrialized nations as their only hope, for if they do they are likely to be disappointed.

For the people of the industrialized nations the first step toward helping the people of the Sahel is to understand their plight—that their misery is not merely the result of nature gone mad but of past and present history as well. Actions will follow from that understanding.

COPING WITH FAMINE [5]

Never throughout history has there been a time when there has not been a devastating famine in some part of the world. In our lifetime, widespread starvation in Asia, Europe, Africa and Latin America has taken the lives of millions of men, women and children. We know that somewhere, this year, there will be a new famine—the result of war or a major national catastrophe. Already there is starvation in the Sahel area south of the Sahara, and the threat of renewed serious crop failure in the Indian subcontinent. The presently bad—and worsening—state of the total world food supply, particularly the depletion of grain reserves in the United States and the shortage of the fertilizers needed to maintain the "green revolution" as a result of high oil prices, leads one to expect that the extent of any new famine will indeed be catastrophic. Historically we have proved ourselves ill-prepared to cope with famines. How well can we hope to deal with them in an even less propitious situation?

Up to now, individual nations, international voluntary agencies, and especially official international organizations have dealt with the specter of mass starvation as an unexpected crisis—as something to react to when it occurs rather than as a likelihood to be planned for in advance. Prevention has been the exception rather than the rule; Bihar in 1966–67, to be discussed later, remains the lone shining example of a large famine averted. Moreover, we act on the occasion of each famine as though mankind had no collective memory. Whoever is faced with the present famine usually acts as though there were no lesson to be derived from the melancholy succession of previous famines and previous efforts to cope with them.

Yet previous famines should have left one beneficial

[5] From article by Jean Mayer, professor of nutrition, Harvard University. *Foreign Affairs*. 53:98-120. O. '74. Excerpted by permission from *Foreign Affairs*, October 1974. Copyright 1974 by Council on Foreign Relations, Inc.

residue: there are individuals and organizations that have acquired firsthand knowledge of successful—and unsuccessful—ways of coping. So little is ordinarily taught of the physiological, psychological and social problems arising in famines, and of their solutions, however, that each new group of physicians and administrators who are generally called upon to deal with a new catastrophic situation tends to repeat some of the classic errors of omission and commission.

Today, we need, and are technically able to create, an organization that institutionalizes human memory in dealing with starvation. Over time we have made discoveries in compassion as well as in management and technology. For many centuries starvation was essentially inevitable, largely because means of information and means of transportation were not at hand. That there was some food somewhere else on the same or another continent was basically irrelevant: there was no way of delivering it when it was needed or of distributing it to the starving. We now have the technology to keep the whole world under surveillance and transmit early warnings of impending shortages; we can transport the food to the area of famine. Therefore we have obligations that did not exist in past generations.

For action purposes there is a sharp difference between a state of chronic starvation, which is endemic in some sections of certain populations, and a true famine. However precarious their previous state of nutrition may have been, the people involved feel and act differently in a famine; they become acutely conscious that something of a different order of magnitude is happening.

A true famine is unlike anything else. It can be defined as a severe shortage of food accompanied by a significant increase in the local or regional death rate. In a chronic starvation area people may suffer and be crippled mentally and physically; in a true famine they die in large numbers.

Almost all recorded famines have resulted from widespread crop failures. These, in turn, may be caused by drought, crop diseases or pests, the impact of war or civil disturbance, or a combination of disturbances hitting both crops and farmers, such as floods or earthquakes. All these four sets of causes have been at work in the famines that have occurred since 1950 alone: flood, drought and civil disorder in India and Pakistan; locusts and earthquakes in the Middle East; floods and dislocation of the agricultural system in China; earthquakes in Latin America (including the recent Peruvian disaster); and drought and civil war in Africa (the Sahel, the Congo and Biafra).

All of the causes of crop failure and famine are very much alive in the world today. The most threatening, and growing, is now drought. Some scientists are saying that changes in climate have shortened the growing season and reduced the rainfall that we may now expect in key areas such as India and northern Africa. Whether this is true or not, the large areas of the world where rainfall is highly variable and seasonal are inherently drought-prone. In Western Europe or New England a dry year differs from a wet year by less than 20 percent; in immense land areas elsewhere, the variation may be 80 percent, and drought years may alternate with years of flood, when gigantic continental rivers, swollen by excessive rains in the mountains, burst their banks and destroy all crops.

Apart from their climate and natural characteristics, many nations and areas are particularly vulnerable to famine by reason of lack of communications or social inequality. Chinese famines of the past were due largely to the then primitive transportation system, and lack of adequate communication is a major aspect of the current Sahel famine. These problems exist in many poor countries. Virtually all such countries are examples of social inequality and of the resulting defects in nutrition for large sections of the population. It may be useful to remember that in as rich a country as Britain in 1935, with an average intake of 2,000 calories daily, at least 10 percent of the population was underfed to the point of growth retardation, and 40 percent ate a diet that was demonstrably too low in certain vitamins. Obviously, in a country like Egypt, where biblical farming methods can still be seen in operation not many miles from the modern capital, social inequalities and malnutrition are even more acute.

To move from causes to consequences, by the above definition the main and most immediate effect of famine is widespread deaths from starvation. The number of deaths is a good index of the severity of the famine, and conversely a drop in that number an index of the effectiveness of the measures employed in combatting it. It has been observed repeatedly that in famines old persons and young children die first, and that women and adolescents tend to survive better than men (although adolescents suffering from prolonged undernutrition are particularly susceptible to tuberculosis). For purposes of dealing with a famine, "old age" starts at about forty-five years old. From then on, there is a drastic increase in mortality as compared with adult men and women below that age.

A second, and dangerous, consequence is the state of social disruption, including large-scale panics, that usually accompanies a famine. Generally people who are starving at home tend to leave it if they can and march toward the area where food is rumored to be available. As a result, families are separated and children are lost. The small children often reach a suicidal state of mind from self-inflicted starvation, refusing to eat because of their grief at the absence of their parents. Adolescents, finding themselves on their own, band together in foraging gangs that create further disruption. (Prolonged and successful practice of banditry also makes members of these gangs difficult to rehabilitate when the famine is over.) This breakdown of the social order makes any relief measure that much harder to put into effect.

Contrary to popular belief, however, famines (and, for that matter, prolonged severe undernutrition) are rarely accompanied by revolution. The gravely underfed usually are too feeble and too preoccupied with problems of immediate survival to summon up the energy, single-mindedness and organization required to initiate and follow through with a revolution. . . .

A third common catastrophic result of famines is the spread of epidemics. The combination of physiologically weakened human organisms and a disrupted social organism, with the attendant breakdown of public-health institutions and crowding, lends itself to the explosive spread of infectious diseases. Louse-borne typhus has been the traditional post-famine disease of Europe, cholera and smallpox the post-famine diseases in Asia, although plague, influenza, tuberculosis, relapsing fever, and many other diseases have also followed famine. When famine is due to a drought, malaria is not usually rampant at the same time, but is often deadly on a particularly large scale when the rains finally come.

One last, long-term, consequence of many famines is the death of large domestic animals, often on a greater scale than that of humans, and the destruction of seeds for future crops, making it more difficult for farming to return to normal when the famine is over. (The Sahel famine is the most recent example of both points.) If one is to speak of coping with famine, one must include follow-on measures to restore the food supply and rehabilitate the area—or if this cannot be done, to resettle the population elsewhere. . . .

A fine example of coping with and containing a famine was the national and international effort during the famine in India during 1966–67. What the Indian Ministry of Food and Agriculture feared would be "a natural calamity of a magnitude unknown in recent times" became instead the object of what the Washington *Post* later described as "one of the biggest and most successful relief operations ever undertaken." Of all the subcontinent, the eastern Indian state of Bihar was most affected by the drought and subsequent famine, and it was here that the relief activities were concentrated.

Bihar had at that time the second largest population of the Indian states—roughly equivalent to that of France. Its economy was, and is, almost entirely agricultural; about nine tenths of its 52 million people were engaged in farming, and of the 27 million acres in crops, less than one fifth were irrigated, and of these only about 7 percent from sure sources. While Bihar sits on one of the world's largest reservoirs of ground water, digging of wells and irrigation schemes had been postponed or delayed for almost a decade; when the monsoon failed for two years in a row, crop failure was inevitable. Over the two-year period, Bihar fell short of needed grain by almost 30 million tons. Reserves of food grains, including those necessary for seeds, had been mostly consumed; the crop of the fall before was at best one fourth of normal, the spring crop only one half. In addition, the Bihar state's administrative apparatus was relatively unsophisticated, and it had no child-feeding program which could have been used as the base of a relief effort.

However, when the famine began, there were some bright spots. During the lesser drought of the previous year, the Indian government had set up fair-price shops and practiced the logistics of importing and transporting large quantities of grain; voluntary agencies had acquired experience in setting up mass feeding programs. Bihar itself had adequate storage and transportation facilities and an administrative structure that lent itself, especially in the Education Department, to relief operations. Moreover, ever since British times the Indian government had placed in the hands of its officials a comprehensive elementary guide to the handling of famines, called a Famine Code.

The basic priority of the Indian government was to obtain and dispense sufficient food. For this, three outlets were used: twenty thousand fair-price shops distributed grain at fixed, subsidized prices; ten ounces of free grain were distributed each day to each aged or infirm person; and a child-feeding program provided one free meal each day to six million children and mothers. Members of the government, vividly aware, some of them for the first time, of the long-term personal and social effects of malnutrition, not only tended to favor the children in relief programs, but also speeded the development of a cereal-based, high-protein food, Bak Ahar, processed and packaged by Indian industry and distributed by the Indian government.

In the Bihar famine, the need for water was as great as the need for food. Lack of water threatened to cause the mass migration of villagers, thus destroying the food distribution system, in addition to posing health hazards in the hottest months of the year. To meet this need, the government began a program of well-drilling—some of the wells to be permanent, the rest of a more temporary nature, but each providing drinking water and irrigating half an acre of land through the driest period of the summer. Further needs for water were met by establishing an elaborate transport system, comprising modes of travel from railways to bullock carts.

Remembering the high death toll from cholera and smallpox during the Bengal famine of 1943, the government also disinfected wells and set up an immunization program. The response of the American government to the Indian request for vaccine, incidentally, was a model of promptness and efficiency—vaccine, injectors, and inoculation specialists to train Indians in their use arrived at Delhi five days after the formal request was made.

The government set up an information network that transmitted data by telephone or telegraph to a master control room where they were charted to give day-to-day information on food stocks and prices, water levels, disease rates and deaths, the numbers of people at free kitchens and on work projects, even the rate of local food looting. From this control center, field workers and the population were kept abreast of the changing situation by short-wave and public radio.

In addition, the government undertook to provide millions of dollars in loans to the Bihari farmers for the purchase of seeds, fertilizers, pesticides, and farm animals to rejuvenate the economy and prepare for the 1967–68 crop.

In all these efforts, the local Bihari government and the federal government of India were supported by supplies and cooperation from other nations, the United Nations, and international voluntary organizations. CARE alone set up 27,000 school feeding centers in Bihar to provide free meals to children and nursing mothers; the United States contributed one fifth of its wheat crop.

In the end, the famine was contained. Instead of the millions of deaths predicted, the highest of the fairly reliable estimates was only a few thousand. It appears that among the poorest segments of society many were better fed during the famine than before—or perhaps afterward. The success of the emergency feeding program, especially in the health of the Bihari children (they were fed milk, and foods and food supplements high in protein, iron and other minerals, as well as vitamins, under fairly close supervision), led to a long-term commitment by the Indian government to the nutritional needs of the population. Even the work program, which certainly resulted, in some cases, in roads leading to and from nowhere, also sparked projects for more and better irrigation, field leveling, more efficient farming methods with higher yields, and better water conservation.

Despite the resolve of the Indian government to fight this famine with every possible resource, however, the struggle would have been hopeless without the dedicated cooperation of the international community. . . .

We should not leave a discussion of recent famines without at least a brief notice of the worst of all—the situation in which war is the cause, and where one or more of the combatants may argue that it is an "internal matter." In such cases the humanitarian instincts of the international community may be dulled by political motives. There is essentially no chance, under the present conventions of international behavior, for a war-related famine to end anything but tragically. . . .

The famines in Biafra [in Nigeria] and in 1972 in Bangladesh are of very recent memory. In the case of Bangladesh, the government itself, although new and untried, did relatively well at coping with the situation, in spite of the disorganization and disruption caused by the war [for independence from Pakistan]. The expertise of the Indian government was also a big factor. International aid to Bangladesh was hampered by the fact that more than one government was involved, each with its own foreign policies to protect or further. The US government did relatively well with its relief effort, but while it was useful, it was in this case not really a deciding factor.

Biafra was a more difficult situation. Although the Biafrans had their own territory and government, the international community persisted in considering their rebellion, at least officially, as an internal affair of the Nigerians. The United States, fearing that giving aid to the Biafrans, even for famine relief, would be considered a hostile act by the Nigerians, gave food through UNICEF and the Red Cross, but tried not to be involved. Although the Biafran government was competent and attacked the problem with organization and imagination, there was little it could do against the Nigerian blockade and the indifference of other nations.

As one who was closely involved in the relief effort, I can state that much more could have been done had the United States and other national governments not lacked the courage. Even most of the UN organizations, in particular FAO and WHO [World Health Organization], were as afraid of interfering as the United States. Indeed, in some instances they went to fantastic extremes not to be involved. UNICEF, alone of the UN organizations, worked without favor on both sides of the battle lines. And it is interesting and, I hope, instructive, that as a result it now has increased prestige and popularity throughout Nigeria, and elsewhere. This is a deserved tribute to the mixture of courage and goodwill that should have been uppermost in the entire international community even during a civil war.

Bangladesh is independent, Nigeria is at peace. Yet surely we need not repeat either of these man-made catastrophes.

While all men of goodwill recognize the need to outlaw chemical and biological warfare, is this enough? Both of these are indiscriminate in their effects, jeopardizing civilian bystanders as much as they do armed enemies. I would like to propose that starvation be similarly outlawed as a legitimate instrument of war, on the ground that it is worse than indiscriminate: it preferentially attacks small children, pregnant and nursing women, and the elderly.

The facts are that young, adult men are physiologically the most resistant to starvation, and that armed men rarely starve, particularly as they can always justify their requisitions by the nobility of their cause.

An international agreement to outlaw starvation as a weapon of war should be supplemented by one empowering suitable international organizations, such as UNICEF, the Food and Agriculture Organization, or the World Health Organization, to enter a famine area to feed the noncombatant victims of starvation without prior authorization. How many large-scale disasters do we need before we learn that famine and pestilence are not purely "internal problems"? The time has come when, through international agreement and action, man-created famines should be eliminated. Any use of starvation as a means of pressure or punishment against individuals in small or large population groups is a violation of the rights of man.

III. THE GREEN REVOLUTION AND BEYOND

EDITOR'S INTRODUCTION

The past two decades in America witnessed any number of "revolutionary" movements—often accompanied by divisions within our society and even violence—movements sparked by civil rights advocates, student militants, Vietnam protesters, feminist leaders, American Indian activists. Among the slogans of this era, there was one with a thoroughly peaceful and harmonious overtone—the green revolution, which refers to the adoption of advanced scientific growing techniques in areas of the world previously lacking self-sufficiency in food production.

How "revolutionary" these new steps are and the extent of their permanent effect is still a matter of debate. In this section, varying aspects of the green revolution are examined in three articles: a review of the work of Dr. Norman E. Borlaug and his associates; a critical survey by Professor Cecil W. Smith; and a report of progress in rice production in the Philippines by Professor Robert Huke.

Dr. David Grigg next examines farming in the less developed countries in a general historical setting. There follows an optimistic view of farming progress in the Negev desert of Israel by Peter Bunyard.

Next there is a brief description of what is both a new and a traditional source of food—the lakes, rivers, and oceans around us. Fish and seafood have long provided protein nourishment. The new aspect deals with fish "farming," the cultivation of fish on a controlled basis. Finally, a *Farm Journal* article describes new research programs designed to improve the world's agricultural productivity.

BORLAUG AND THE GREEN REVOLUTION [1]

One morning in late February [1975], Dr. Norman E. Borlaug, the Iowa farmer and plant pathologist who won the 1970 Nobel Peace Prize, arose at 6:00 in the Costa de Oro Motel in Ciudad Obregón, in northwestern Mexico, pulled on his khaki trousers and work boots and walked to the motel coffee shop. There he swapped gossip with the local farmers who gather there each morning, and downed his customary breakfast of *huevos rancheros* [ranch-style eggs with a hot sauce]. Finished, he put on his baseball cap (Borlaug introduced Little League baseball to Mexico, and proudly sports the cap of the Mexico City Aztecas, the last all-star team he coached), and walked to his Chevrolet in the shortened, splay-footed gait he has acquired from a lifetime of navigating the U-shaped furrows of plowed fields.

Borlaug's dedication to agriculture has always been intense to the point of fanaticism; his involvement with baseball was urged upon him years ago by a colleague who perceived that Borlaug was suffering from overwork and exhaustion. Almost single-handed, Borlaug has been responsible for quadrupling the production of wheat in Mexico since 1950, for more than doubling wheat output in both India and Pakistan between 1968 and 1972, and for working out techniques of breeding, fertilization and irrigation that have since been applied to rice and other crops in a broad but now controversial movement known as the green revolution.

The green revolution refers to the effort that began about a decade ago to stimulate agriculture in developing nations through the use of high-yielding varieties of grains—especially wheat and rice. The varieties usually have short, stiff stalks, respond quickly to fertilizer and resist common plant diseases. Their proper cultivation usually requires

[1] From "The Green Revolution Lives," by Alan Anderson, Jr., freelance writer. New York *Times Magazine.* p 15+. Ap. 27, '75. © 1975 by The New York Times Company. Reprinted by permission.

insecticides, pesticides and irrigation, in addition to fertilizer and good farming practices. The earliest successes of the grains came in Mexico, a nation that moved from large-scale wheat importing to self-sufficiency to modest exporting in less than fifteen years. The most dramatic leap forward came in India and Pakistan, where the green revolution produced its first headlines. Before the advent of green revolution wheat in India, most farmers would expect to harvest about 1 metric ton of wheat and 1.5 tons of rice per year per hectare [2.47 acres]. With the new grains, fertilizer and good farm management, the same farmer saw his harvest soar to 5 tons of wheat and 7 tons of rice per hectare. Lesser, but increasing gains in wheat yields were under way in Iran, Turkey, Jordan, Syria, Egypt, Libya, Tunisia, mainland China and dozens of other developing countries. New rice varieties were pushing up yields in the Philippines, Thailand, Bangladesh, India and elsewhere in Asia.

In 1972, however, the movement was staggered by a succession of blows. The Ukrainian wheat crop failed, and crafty Russian traders subsequently pulled off the biggest Chicago grain purchase in history, leading to the sudden disappearance of grain reserves in North America. A worldwide fertilizer shortage developed, as consumption began to outpace production, and the situation was aggravated by the Arab oil embargo (nitrogen fertilizer is made from petroleum products). Worldwide inflation did not help, nor did an epidemic of bad weather that continued through 1973 and 1974. In a period of two years, wheat prices rose 250 percent, rice prices 300 percent and fertilizer prices as much as 700 percent. It became painfully clear during those years, too, that whatever the successes of the green revolution, they were not enough to prevent starvation in areas of drought or continued population explosion, and predictions of dire food shortages grew common.

In the meantime, Borlaug and his work had become the focus of controversy as well as acclaim. Though Borlaug had made an immense contribution to alleviating the food-population crises, the world could not simply accept it for what it was. Borlaug and his revolution, critics charged, raised the false hope that technology could continue indefinitely to increase crop yields as fast as humans are producing more humans. They also argued that the green revolution was moving the world toward dependence on a few highly specialized varieties, thereby increasing the risk of catastrophic crop failures because of disease, and that these specialized varieties were forcing the world's farmers to become too dependent on fertilizer. And some faulted Borlaug for developing a farming approach that seemed best suited to wealthy owners of large farms rather than poor peasants. The central, urgent question of how to provide enough food for the hungry seemed to grow obscure behind a welter of social and political issues. . . .

Borlaug was sent to Mexico as an unusual form of foreign aid. Just before World War II, the Mexican Government sent the United States an official plea for economic help. The Rockefeller Foundation was asked to respond to the agricultural segment of the plea, and Borlaug was part of that response. Soon after his arrival in 1944, he was charged with boosting wheat production, which was in a piteous state. The average national yield was only 750 kilograms per hectare, or 11 bushels per acre; wheat fields in the United States today commonly yield 10 times as much. Virtually no research was being done on wheat breeding, fertilization, disease resistance or irrigation. Popular demand for bread was growing, forcing the nation to import 55 percent of its wheat at an annual cost of $21 million. The foreign exchange currency was desperately needed for farm machinery and fertilizer. In Mexico, as in most tropical regions, population was beginning the slow explosion that continues today; almost without exception, however, governments were totally neglecting agricultural research in favor of industrial expansion. The Rockefeller team quickly saw that food production must be stimulated fairly quickly, and that the logical place to begin was with the cereals.

Cereals, or grains, as they are commonly called, are the fruits of cultivated grasses—enlarged and pampered versions of what a suburbanite would see if his lawn were allowed to go to seed. Grains are the single most important component of the world's food supply, and the most widely grown types in the world are wheat, rice, maize, barley, millet, oats and rye.

Wheat is by far the most important of the world's grains. It is nourishing, adaptable, and easy to grow. Its taste is mild, and it can be stored for many years or shipped easily around the world. The protein of wheat, gluten, has an elastic quality unique among grains. Because of this elasticity, wheat dough is able to hold the tiny gas bubbles emitted by yeast during fermentation, so that light, fluffy bread can be produced from wheat flour.

Borlaug realized that three major obstacles stood between Mexican farmers and good wheat crops: First, during moist periods, the plants were helpless against rust fungus; second, no single variety of wheat could grow in Mexico's diverse climatic regions and, third, although the wheats yielded poorly, fertilizer caused them to grow top-heavy and "lodge," or fall over, before harvest time. He reasoned that solutions lay in selective breeding—the development of varieties with favorable genes, such as those for high yield, disease-resistance and the ability to flourish in a wide range of environments. Such breeding amounts to a process of trial and error, repeated over and over. . . .

Wheat, like nearly all grains except corn, is by nature a self-pollinating plant: Every head of wheat bears sixty or more flowers, each complete with both male and female parts, and without interference, each plant bears offspring that are faithful copies of the parent. Interference, however, is the name of the breeding game, a wearying and muscle cramping operation central to the entire CIMMYT [Mexican acronym for International Wheat and Maize Improvement Center] program. Seated motionless on a three-legged stool, the breeder must carefully remove the pollen-produc-

ing anther from each flower of each plant that is to be a
female. This "emasculation" prevents self-fertilization, creating a "cow" which must be carefully covered with a paper
envelope to prevent accidental pollination by another plant.
For each cow, a bull is selected on the basis of some desirable trait, such as disease resistance, straw strength, or good
milling and baking qualities. When both bull and cow are
ripe, the head is severed from the bull, brought to the cow,
and twirled quickly inside the protecting envelope. This
scatters pollen over the sixty or more ovaries. . . .

The second breakthrough was the breeding of varieties
that can be planted at any time of year. Borlaug was baffled
by the failure of Canadian wheats to grow in Mexico. After
much testing, colleagues discovered that the problem lay in
photosensitivity: The plants were genetically sensitized to
the long daylight of northern summers. The researchers began shuttling wheats north and south between Obregón and
Mexico City, 10 degrees apart in latitude. By selecting
plants that thrived in both places, they developed varieties
without genes for photosensitivity. These photosensitive
wheats were capable of growing at any latitude. In addition,
the shuttle achieved an extra goal: Any varieties that suc-
ceeded in both the hot fields of Obregón near sea level and
in the cooler southern fields at an altitude of 8,500 feet
showed themselves to be hardy enough to flourish in widely
different environments. . . .

Through the late 1940s and early fifties, Borlaug spent
all his time crossing wheats. Improvements came quickly,
but the tradition-bound farmers were skeptical, and refused
to try the new seeds. When he was able to point to rich
demonstration fields, however, and talk to the farmers in
terms of pesos and centavos, they began to listen. By the
mid-fifties, the new wheats were catching on, and by 1956
Mexico was self-sufficient in wheat, as she has been ever
since. Even greater yield increases came with the introduction of dwarf wheats, developed in the state of Washington
in the 1950s by Dr. Orville Vogel—short, stiff-stalked plants

that could be fertilized heavily without lodging. By 1962, Mexico was releasing its own tropical dwarfs, and yields leaped from 4.5 tons per hectare to 6-7 and even 8 tons per hectare. Demand for the dwarf seed was so brisk that black markets flourished for years; the same thing happened later in India and Pakistan.

While CIMMYT licked the problem of low yield early on, it is still locked in battle with a dizzying range of wheat diseases. . . .

Despite the obvious achievements of the green revolution, Borlaug and his colleagues are well aware of the bad press that has been stirred up by the setbacks of the last few years. . . . I asked him about an article in *Fortune,* which charged that "the price that has been paid for the high productivity may be a lack of adaptability." He grunted, and took a sip of a margarita.

You'll see a lot of nonsense that we are becoming susceptible to disease because we are just growing a few varieties. But those few varieties are the result of so many crosses made within our program and in affiliated countries that there is tremendous built-in resistance. More genetic variability is being put into grains now than ever before in the history of the world.

Well, I went on, what about the charge that green revolution grains are "addicted" to large diets of fertilizer, without which they are even less productive than native varieties? Again, his answer was blunt.

People are always asking us to develop a kind of grain that doesn't need fertilizer. All right, I say, I'll have that grain for you six months or a year after you develop a man or woman who doesn't need to eat. Once you've established the principle, I can apply it to grains.

. . . I also relayed the charge that the green revolution is helping only large farmers.

Our goal [said Elmer Johnson, who is trying to do for corn what has been done for wheat and rice] is to produce something that will grow in poor countries and will reach the small farmers. But this isn't easy where there are no national programs to communicate with the farmer. We can't give him seed if he doesn't know about it. We can't give him fertilizer unless someone can pay for it. We can't give him a tractor if his land isn't big enough to turn a tractor around on. In some countries, the agricultural engineers don't even know what the small farmers are growing.

So far, the corn breeders at CIMMYT have reduced the height of native corn by about a meter, and are patiently trying to introduce a gene for high-quality protein into popular varieties. . . .

Borlaug showed me the most exciting triumph of the CIMMYT breeding program: triticale, the world's first man-made cereal. Triticale (tri-ti-KAY-lee), a cross between wheat *(Triticum)* and rye *(Secale)*, combines the high yield of wheat with the extreme hardiness and disease resistance of rye. In the beginning, the chief obstacle was lack of fertility: By natural laws, crosses between different species are usually sterile, like a mule. But by genetic accident . . . a triticale "mule" managed to cross with a dwarf of wheat. Triticale goes into semicommercial production . . . [in 1975] in the central highlands of Mexico. In Texas and California, there are already more than a dozen triticale products on the market including Tritiflakes, Triticakes and Triti-pizza. . . .

The most exciting goal at the moment is a long-dreamed-of "super cereal" combining the high yielding ability of a cereal with the legume. Soybeans and other legumes grow in symbiosis with colonies of bacteria that possess the priceless ability to "fix" nitrogen, or convert it from the free, gaseous state into solid nitrogen compounds that can be used by plants to build proteins and other essential chemicals. A cereal that could fix its own nitrogen would manufacture much of its own fertilizer, skirt the energy crisis and save farmers hundreds of thousands of dollars a year. . . .

Some critics of the green revolution say that its very goal is inappropriate: Greater food production will increase the number of people who must eventually starve. . . .

"What we need more than anything," said Borlaug,

banging his fist on the table, "is the will and commitment of governments to support dedicated agricultural scientists as leaders. And these leaders have got to go out into the field with the farmers. If we can't get the green revolution to the little guy, there is no revolution." . . .

GREEN REVOLUTION:
PROMISES AND PROBLEMS [2]

To what extent is the green revolution—a massive world-wide effort to increase food production that began nearly thirty years ago—producing more rhetoric than it is wheat and rice? To be sure, impressive results have been achieved over the years in many parts of the world, and many people believe that virtually all the answers to the questions of achieving high agricultural output have been found. Closer examination of the phenomenon called the green revolution reveals, however, that the term *revolution* can be applied only to about 10 or 15 percent of the agricultural lands in Asia and to much lesser proportions in Africa and Latin America. Furthermore, a whole series of problems has arisen in connection with the great thrusts in agricultural development. These problems go far beyond those of selecting the optimum insecticide or the most adaptable wheat species; they affect almost every segment of the societies in which the green revolution seeks a foothold.

The importance of the green revolution and the urgency of its being successful should be obvious. In order to meet even partially the nutritional requirements of the 6 to 7 billion people expected on our planet in the year 2000, developed and developing lands must continue and expand their cooperative agricultural development efforts. . . .

Efforts started by the Rockefeller Foundation in co-operation with the government of Mexico during the 1940s

[2] From "Promises and Problems of the Green Revolution," by Cecil N. Smith, professor of food and resource economics, University of Florida. *Economic Leaflets* (University of Florida Bureau of Economic and Business Research). 31:1-4. Ag.-S. '72.

to increase production of corn and wheat constitute the origin of what is now popularly called the green revolution. New and improved varieties of grains—especially rice and wheat—and associated modern inputs (fertilizer, pesticides, financial and technical assistance and sometimes mechanization and irrigation) enabled farmers in many parts of the developing world to achieve large increases in production. The green revolution, in effect, has facilitated the substitution of fertilizer for land. Nevertheless, this "revolution" has been adopted by only a small segment of farmers. Many side effects have affected other segments of the economies of the third world. Despite the rapid progress in the green revolution which has been achieved . . . , there appears to be almost general agreement that substantial further advances will be fraught with a host of difficulties.

Many of these so-called "second generation" problems involve inadequate pricing and marketing policies as well as the lack of specific production aids, such as improved seeds and insecticides. These problems are formidable, but they are largely short-run issues in which scientists have a substantial background of experience. By contrast, the "third generation" problems, which involve equity, welfare, employment, environment and social institutions, have received inadequate attention even in the developed countries. Third generation problems are rising from four major sources: (1) very high population growth rates in areas which are already extremely densely populated; (2) very low average income levels, coupled simultaneously with great regional and personal variations in income, wealth and political power; (3) limited new or additional opportunities for nonfarm and farm employment even if the manufacturing and service sectors grow very rapidly; and (4) the possibility of technological leap-frogging in agriculture with inputs and techniques which are often of a labor-displacing nature. . . .

Adjustments in Economic Systems

Increased food-grain production with the new rice, corn and wheat varieties has brought about a whole series of pressures within the economic systems of the countries where these increases have occurred. Relatively few policy decisions were made soon enough by governments and by those portions of the private and public sectors concerned with the handling and marketing of grains. One key problem has been transportation bottlenecks. For example, in Sind, Pakistan, the railway system was unable to haul the additional supplies of rice produced in 1969. Large quantities were piled up at rail centers, where storage was lacking, and prices received by farmers dropped considerably. The milling system was also not prepared to cope with the large increases in supplies.

When a developing country has traditionally sustained food deficits and a price policy with little or no relationship to world prices for a commodity, the changes it faces as it shifts to self-sufficiency and then to surplus production may be astounding. Tremendous problems arise when a country has a price level which may be half again or double the level of world prices. Major adjustments which may have adverse economic, social and political implications for various groups must take place.

Some of the green revolution grain varieties have met consumer resistance in the marketplace. This causes problems not only for farmers, but also for all sectors of the marketing system and for policy makers. However, it is likely that most of these consumer acceptance problems are of a short-run nature. Many of the most severe quality problems will undoubtedly be solved by new strains and varieties which the geneticists and agronomists are developing and testing.

Economic Development

Any form of economic development, including that in agriculture, often tends to be destabilizing in character. The problem of growth and equity in countries experiencing the green revolution is one for which solutions cannot be found by the agricultural sector alone. The solution requires increased savings, more foreign exchange, high rates of investment and altered factor and product pricing structures—in brief, economic development. Agricultural development through the green revolution can contribute to economic development, but answers to overall national problems must be found in other sectors of the economy as well. . . .

Labor and Agriculture

Even with the rapid expansion of industry and service activities in their economies, it appears that jobs for people displaced from farms in India, Pakistan, Indonesia and other developing societies will lag behind the rapid increase in population.

Solutions to unemployment problems in developing countries are essential to future development and stability. Increasing agribusiness and other employment opportunities on the farms and rural areas, for example, may be one solution for people to make effective contributions to their societies and have the purchasing power to buy its products. Already cities like Calcutta, Rio de Janeiro, Bogota and many others are plagued by problems of unemployment, extremely poor housing, dire malnutrition and suffering on the part of many people who migrated from rural areas. . . .

Environmental Problems

The United Nations Conference on the Human Environment held . . . [in 1971] in Stockholm has called attention to the problems of man and the continued use of his environment for his improved welfare. Representatives of many developing countries voiced their beliefs that limitations on the use of their resources will be to their extreme disadvantage at the present time. Nevertheless, environmental problems such as pesticide residues, air and water pollution and others, which are now plaguing the developed countries are appearing in the developing lands and will doubtless limit growth, including that in agriculture and the progress of the green revolution. In all too many instances nature has been abused beyond its limits. Whether in developed or developing countries, revenge is inevitable when this occurs.

The environmental problem is likely to emerge as one of the most troublesome aspects of future international relations. Pollutants, for example, cannot be confined to their source, but are carried freely by wind currents and through food chains regardless of political boundaries. Despite its biological complexity, however, the environmental issue is even more intricate on the political level because of its very close relationship with health and survival. Many nations, including the developed ones, are realizing that pollution, despoilization and degradation are not isolated in themselves but are the dark side of progress, prosperity and development. Inaction in one area has consequences in another. . . .

Welfare and Stability

Another disturbing element of the green revolution concerns side effects on welfare and stability. These are basically related to the unequal patterns of growth in various regions which are directly related to the new technology utilized in the green revolution. For example, areas such as the Punjab in India and Pakistan which have irrigation, have been able to respond very rapidly to the new technology. The rapid growth in such areas contributes to larger food supplies, expanded development and spurts in the national product. The problem is that standards of living between regions as well as among people tend to be more relative than absolute concepts. Thus, without tremendous shifts in taxation, welfare and other development programs, such very rapid growth may tend to have a destabilizing influence.

Those farmers who have reaped the benefits of the green revolution and who have had access to irrigation facilities have generally been large operators. Their incomes have risen very rapidly. The writer does not believe this to be bad. Nevertheless, many of the side effects may be undesirable. For example, land prices tend to rise very rapidly as farmers seek new outlets for their increasing income by expanding the size of their operations. In addition, the gains accruing to these farmers tend to bring about certain types of mechanization. Some may displace labor. One of the net results will probably be to increase the inequality of income of people. Increased tension among various groups and classes of people may well be an end product. . . .

Prospect

The green revolution has achieved substantial progress toward increasing the production of food in many of the world's developing nations. To defuse the "food-population" time bomb which is burning at a terrific rate of speed, strong measures must also be taken to stem the population explosion. In the short run the United States and other nations with food surpluses can supply limited stocks of food as well as fertilizer and other key inputs. Changes in the trade and production policies of developed nations can also do much to foster the balanced growth of developing nations. However, the technical assistance in agricultural development which is proffered will be effective only when there is a will on the part of recipient nations to adopt it.

Long-run solutions, including adjustments to the social, political and economic problems which accompany advances in agricultural productivity, lie with the people of the developing societies. Whether or not these people succeed in producing more food—and in improving the nutrition, which generally depends on more equally distributed incomes—for their exploding population is of prime concern to all who inhabit this planet.

SAN BARTOLOME AND
THE GREEN REVOLUTION [3]

Farmers in the developing world have not been thought
of as holding progressive attitudes toward innovation, and
agricultural settlements have not often been regarded as
foci of change. In fact, farm villages have long been regarded as the last sector of the economy to accept modernization, and the blame has frequently been placed on the
farmer himself who has been accused as a reactionary who
lives so close to the margin that he is forced to stick with
traditional patterns of production because he dares not risk
the failure which might result from change.

Fortunately such generalizations are not always true.
San Bartolome, Mayantoc, Tarlac [the Philippines] provides
a case in point. Here is a barrio [rural community unit]
where adoption of modern farming techniques has been
rapid, where evidence of economic change is abundant, and
where attitudes of local farmers are surprisingly progressive.

The Setting

The province of Tarlac has long been known as a melt-
ing pot with one of the greatest mixes of ethnic groups and
languages of any of the provinces of the Philippines. In
Tarlac agriculture is the way of life for the majority of the
population, but farming is not easy here. The work is difficult; the returns are not great. Much of the land in the
province is held by absentee landlords and their 50 percent
share of the produce of a small, overworked farm leaves the
operator with barely enough to feed his family. Throughout
the province palay [rice prior to husking] is clearly the
premier crop, being planted on roughly 80 percent of the
farmed land. It is the farmer's staff of life, the area's chief
item of trade. In days gone by a traveler passing through

[3] From article by Robert E. Huke, professor of geography, chairman of
geography department, Dartmouth College. *Economic Geography.* 50:47-58. Ja. '74.
Reprinted by permission.

the province would have seen field after field of two-meter-tall light green rice plants, each field at almost the same stage of development as its neighbors. Today much of the rice looks dwarfed at a height of only one meter, but what the plants lack in height they appear to have more than made up in density. One further difference, which at first makes little sense at all, is that in the 1970s this short rice appears in a variety of stages of growth. Some fields are ready for harvesting while others are just beginning to head and still others are in the milk stage—a striking difference from the uniformity of a few short years ago. This change results from the fact that the new high-yielding varieties are not responsive to the changing length of daylight hour. Here and there the rice gives way to another tropical grass—the province's second crop, sugarcane—which occupies only one tenth the area planted to rice.

San Bartolome is a barrio in which the farmers have had considerable experience with the new high-yielding varieties of rice. It is also a barrio for which much information on agricultural practices and farm economics is available from detailed surveys. . . .

In 1957 the National Irrigation Administration constructed the Magsaysay Dam, a small concrete diversion dam, on the Camiling River some ten kilometers upstream from San Bartolome. The dam and associated canal system provide irrigation for a wide area including 215 hectares of rice land in San Bartolome. Because the dam provides almost no storage capacity and because the river regime shows wide fluctuation of flow from season to season, the irrigation system cannot provide year-round water supplies to all of the land served by the system. The irrigation water supplied to San Bartolome is considered adequate and reliable during every rainy season, but the system can provide adequate dry-season water to only one-half of the total area served. Accordingly, San Bartolome has dry-season water during even-numbered years while the supply is directed to the opposite side of the Camiling River during odd-numbered years. Thus, farmers served by the NIA system in San Bartolome have traditionally been able to produce three rice crops every two calendar years. . . .

Diffusion

During May and June of 1966 government agencies, a private fertilizer manufacturer, and the International Rice Research Institute [IRRI] all made IR-8 seed available to selected farmers in the municipality of Mayantoc. Local farm management technicians selected farmers who were considered to be important community leaders, among the most successful farmers, and persons with the interest and the resources necessary to multiply the seed effectively. The total volume of seed available for the 21 barrios of Mayantoc was 16⅓ cavans which was planted to an area of slightly less than 20 hectares. The vast majority of this seed was planted in two barrios north of San Bartolome and in a third barrio two kilometers to the south and across the Camiling River. Only one farmer in San Bartolome received any seed and he had only 12 kilograms, sufficient to plant approximately one quarter of a hectare.

The field chosen as the demonstration plot in San Bartolome was an irrigated field at the north edge of the barrio, and as it is immediately adjacent to the road leading to the poblacion [settlement] it is one of the most visible fields in the barrio. The planting was supervised by the resident agriculture extension worker, checked on three times during the growing season by IRRI personnel, and well cared for by the farmer. The weather was normal, insect damage was modest, and the yield from this one quarter hectare was 30 cavans. With the average yield per hectare for the barrio being 48 cavans, the rate of 120 cavans per hectare achieved in this demonstration plot of IR-8 was impressive indeed.

Because of the alternate year system, irrigation water was not available in San Bartolome for the dry season of 1966–67. The next available planting time was the main or wet season of 1967. By that date a large number of farmers were convinced that they wanted to try some of the "new rice." Every farmer in the settlement had watched the previous year's demonstration plot with great interest. During that growing season and in the months that followed the resident agricultural extension worker had spent many an evening talking over the advantages and potentials of IR-8 and the even newer IR-5 with his neighbors. Local farmers did not like the shortness of the new varieties as they thought this might make harvesting more difficult; they were also concerned by the fact that the demonstration plot had required far greater care than that devoted to other fields of equal size. The fact that most of this increase in labor was related to improved farming technology rather than being unique to the IRRI variety was not immediately obvious. In particular, the straight-row, equally spaced transplanting technique which had been used in place of the usual random (*waray-waray*) method caused much concern.

On the other hand, the local farmers were much impressed by the high final yield, by the fact that no lodging had taken place, and by the fact that the IR-8 had shown very little loss from either insect damage or disease. The advantages clearly outweighed the perceived disadvantages and most farmers were anxious to plant part of their holdings to the dwarf rice. Few were willing to risk their entire crop area.

Prior to the main planting in 1967 seed for the IRRI varieties was still somewhat scarce; its cost was higher than that of local varieties; and there remained many questions in the farmers' minds about the reliability of this short, heavy-tillering plant type. Despite the apparent problems, the attractiveness of the high potential yields was reason enough for 40 percent of the barrio farmers to plant at least part of their holdings in IRRI seed. As a group this 40 percent risked only one third of their plantings to the new seed, and in aggregate this area equaled 14 percent of the rice area for the barrio. . . . Fine harvests followed and only two years later, in the 1969 wet season, 78 percent of the farmers had adopted the new seeds, planting 44 percent of their total rice area to IRRI varieties. By the 1969 wet season the typical adopting farmer had enough confidence to plant over one half of his land in the new high-yielding varieties.

Impact on Farms

By the 1969–70 planting seasons the impact of dwarf, nonlodging, nitrogen responsive rice varieties was obvious throughout the barrio. During both the wet and the dry season survey results showed a strong increase in the number of farmers using IRRI varieties and in the percent of total crop area devoted to them. Ninety of 99 farmers, for whom reliable data covering both seasons was available, used an IRRI variety for at least part of the planting and no farmer who had used such a variety in an earlier year failed to do so again in at least one season during 1969–70. . . .

Threshing . . . has rapidly been taken over by machines. The first threshing machine available to the farmers at San Bartolome was obtained by the FACOMA in Mayantoc in 1953. This machine was seldom used by the barrio farmers and the vast majority of palay continued to be threshed by carabao. Following the completion of the irrigation dam in 1957, a few farmers began to use the FACOMA machine, but the majority stayed with the traditional methods.

In 1966 an enterprising resident of Mayantoc purchased a used thresher and began to actively sell its services throughout the municipality. Business was so good that the following year a second thresher was obtained and, by the 1969 wet season, San Bartolome alone was served by six threshers owned by three different residents of the municipality. The machines were all of the same variety and of Philippine manufacture. They were powered by a belt take-off from the tractor which pulled the machine from field to field. In normal field operation these machines can each process between 500 and 600 cavans of palay during a 12-

hour day. Only under exceptional circumstances do the owners operate on a 24-hour basis. Such operations were not observed in San Bartolome during the 1969 wet season harvest.

Farmers like the machine threshing because it saves them a great deal of time and labor. Machine threshing is paid for in kind at the rate of 4 percent of palay yield, a rate considered quite modest by the farmers. The barrio council also looks favorably on the use of such machines as the operators pay a tax, in cash and on the spot, of two centavos for every cavan of palay. The threshers also provide employment for a few young men. Operating crews range in size from as few as four men to a maximum of twelve. Mean crew size observed in San Bartolome and neighboring barrios was ten.

One reason for the rapid increase in machine threshing was the increased volume of palay to be threshed once the high-yielding varieties were accepted. Thus, there is clearly some pressure from the machine owners to encourage the further adoption of the newer rice types. . . .

Non-Farm Impact

Land values have shown remarkable increases over the years at San Bartolome. Prices paid for farm land have traditionally been based on the quality as reflected in the "expected yield" of the plot and on the recent history of palay prices. Fifty percent of the farmers own all of the land they farm and an additional 35 percent own at least part of their land. Farm land transfers, except through death and inheritance, have been minimal. However, several pieces have been sold and most farmers have firm perceptions of the price they would be willing to pay if additional land were available. The increase in values has been particularly rapid since the introduction of IRRI varieties. Mean prices have risen from pesos 2,000 per hectare in 1955 to pesos 7,500 per hectare in 1969.

That the shift to higher yielding rice types and the resultant increase in productivity has had a great impact in the barrio is immediately obvious to even the casual visitor. Thirty percent of the homes were completely rebuilt between 1967 and 1970 and are far more substantial than the older bamboo matting homes in the settlement. The average cost for such work, approximately P11,000 per home, clearly represented a major investment on the part of the barrio residents. Next to many of these new homes are very substantial, solid, raised, and well-protected granaries.

In the long run these granaries may be a far more significant indication of a new and progressive attitude on the part of the farmers than are the modern homes or any of the other material innovations obvious throughout the settlement. The granaries provide the farmer with a degree of freedom in marketing that he never before enjoyed. Many of the farmers belong to the Mayantoc cooperative which stores palay for individual members with the intent of averaging the price received by holding the palay off the market when supplies are high and releasing it when supplies are tight. A surprising number of barrio farmers, some of whom are cooperative members, apparently prefer to store and market the palay themselves, thus eliminating even the modest storage charge levied by the cooperative. The fact that farmers are investing in storage facilities and attempting to maximize their selling price is yet another indication of the new attitude prevalent in the Central Plain. Those individual farmers who have accepted the new high-yielding varieties and the associated modern techniques of its cultivation are at the same time anxious to accept other new ideas which may help to make farming a more rewarding way of life than has been the case in the past.

The new attitude is also evident at the next higher level of social organization, that of the barrio council. With the coming of significantly increased yields per unit area and the advent of ever more widespread use of machine threshing, the San Bartolome barrio council, in 1967, made a decision to impose a tax of two centavos per cavan of threshed

palay. The funds were to be used for barrio improvements.
The first tangible results of this policy were the construction
of a cement bandstand in the plaza and the paving of the
entire plaza area. Materials were purchased with the tax
money and the labor was donated by local residents. Once
the work was completed the new plaza assumed the role
of a much stronger focus of barrio social and economic activity than it had ever previously enjoyed. It also functions
as the best site for drying newly harvested palay. . . .

Conclusion

San Bartolome is not an "average" barrio. It has received
more than a normal share of extension effort; it has an
energetic and devoted farm technician; it has a reliable irrigation system; and it has a very high proportion of owner-
operators. With all these advantages, the productivity gains
and the economic change over recent years have been impressive. Barrio farmers are excited about the potential of
the IRRI varieties and anticipate continued progress in the
years ahead.

During the final week of the research project in San
Bartolome a farmer whom I had come to know very well
asked that I take a picture of him and his family to be
framed and hung on the sitting room wall of their new
home. On the appointed day I arrived to find Antonio, his
wife, and seven children all dressed in their best clothes. As
the family lined up in prearranged and formal positions in
front of the house I noted that a political campaign poster
was displayed prominently beside the door. Yes, Antonio,
in his new affluence, had become politically active and could
no longer be counted among the silent peasant minority.

Here was a man who owned his own farm (only two and
one quarter hectares) but it was his. He had been one of the
first in the barrio to plant IR-8, making a small beginning
during the main planting season in 1966. In 1967 he shifted
to IR-5 and put half of his farm in this newest "miracle"
rice and half in a standard native variety. He continued this

pattern during each wet season and during alternate dry seasons until 1970 at which time he abandoned IR-5 in favor of IR-20. He had adopted the use of a complete fertilizer which he applied at the modest rate of 35 kg of nitrogen per hectare; he had also acquired a back-pack sprayer and applied insecticides to his crops on a regular basis. He did all of his own land preparation using a pair of carabao which he had owned for many years, but since 1967, the entire crop had been threshed by machine at a cost to him of only four percent of the yield compared to the ten percent which had been standard for hand threshing. As with many farmers in San Bartolome, Antonio sold all of his IRRI rice and kept only Taiwan and Intan for home use.

Antonio's one-year-old home was completely paid for as was his wife's two-year-old sewing machine. It was with pride in his voice that he told me that he had made good money since he had started raising IR-8, and that he owed nothing to anyone.

Once all had been arranged and the pictures finally taken Antonio offered me a "blue seal" cigarette (imported) and apologized for the fact that his oldest daughter was not available for the sitting. "After all, she is in Manila at College. You know," he continued, "it's too bad IRRI didn't make miracle rice a few years earlier. If they had, my wife and I could have had more children."

With this innocent comment Antonio very neatly encapsulated the heart of the problem. The green revolution holds untold promise for the enrichment of barrio life, but the green revolution alone, without an equal emphasis on family planning or population control, could promote disaster a generation hence. [See Section IV, below.]

FARMING IN THE LESS DEVELOPED COUNTRIES [4]

Most countries of the third world have between one half and three quarters of their working population engaged in agriculture, and a very small proportion in industry, transport or commerce. The developed countries have less than one tenth of their labor force in agriculture, in some cases less than one twentieth. The conclusion too frequently drawn from this is that a poor country can only become rich by concentrating all of its resources on industrialization, leaving the farmers, the bulk of the population, to fend for themselves.

There are two objections to this belief. First, agriculture is not simply a reservoir of labor and capital for the process of industrialization. Many people in the LDCs [less developed countries] still suffer from undernutrition, many more from malnutrition, and the populations continue to grow. More food must be forthcoming and this can only be achieved by radical institutional and technological changes. Further, for many LDCs, crops constitute the bulk of their exports, and greater efficiency in their production is essential if this income is to be maintained. Second, it is often forgotten that the developed countries all experienced remarkable changes in their farming before the first stages of industrialization began. From the seventeenth to the nineteenth centuries the medieval institutions of Western Europe were slowly dismantled and the output of farming substantially increased. New crops such as turnips, clover and potatoes were adopted, more manure was applied and new implements used. These changes allowed agriculture to provide labor for the growing industries without any fall in total output, and indeed in some cases much of the capital for industrial investment also came from the agricultural sector. By the end of the nineteenth century the flow was

[4] From "The Rural Revolution," by David Grigg, reader in geography, University of Sheffield. *Geographical Magazine.* 45:734-9. Jl. '73. Reprinted by permission.

reversed. Agriculture, which had sparked off industrialization, became increasingly dependent upon industry for iron machinery, for cheap fertilizers, for the processing of its goods and for their marketing.

By the early 1960s there was a growing realization both in the countries of the third world and amongst their advisers that agriculture should receive more attention. Indeed, it is extraordinary how low investment was in agriculture in countries where not only was the great bulk of the population dependent on agriculture, but also much of export income came from agricultural products. . . . Agriculture in the LDCs is still backward and inefficient.

The list of reasons is endless. One is farm structure: throughout most of Asia, Africa and Latin America farms are remarkably small, a few hectares [a hectare is slightly less than 2½ acres] at the most. Furthermore they are highly fragmented, being made up of fields scattered at some distance from one another. Not only does the farmer waste time moving from one plot to the next, but the layout increases the difficulties of irrigation, moving fertilizers and controlling plant diseases. Farms are in many cases so small that they cannot provide an adequate income to sustain the family, let alone allow investment in the new inputs such as fertilizers, new seeds and better implements that are essential for change. In spite of the land reform campaigns that have swept much of the third world since 1945, there are still many farmers who rent their land from landlords on iniquitous terms; in densely populated countries with many landless laborers, exorbitant rents can be charged. Not only is the farmer unable to save enough to improve his farm, but he often has to borrow to buy the essentials of everyday life. Interest rates are high and farmers are soon enmeshed in a spiral of debt. Also, in parts of Africa and Asia it is not tenancy that inhibits the spirit of enterprise, but the persistence of communal tenure where the individual is unlikely to put energy or capital into new methods.

Many farmers are still semisubsistent; that is, their first

concern is to provide food for their family and perhaps a small surplus to pay taxes. They are relatively unresponsive to price changes. In many cases farmers are physically isolated from the market. Poor transport conditions mean cash crops cannot be usefully grown; this limits income, investment and improvement.

Some writers discount the importance of economic factors in agricultural change and emphasize social problems stressing, for example, how the prevalence of the extended family and tribal custom preclude individual enterprise; how religious attitudes limit the proper exploitation of livestock; and perhaps most important, how lack of education limits the farmer's horizon and makes him reluctant to change established methods. Thus, attempts to improve livestock kept by the Masai in East Africa have foundered because they and many other African pastoralists keep cattle for the prestige which accrues to sheer numbers; any improvement must adjust cattle numbers to the grazing resources available. The Masai are reluctant to cull their animals so that overgrazing, soil erosion and a further reduction of grazing resources continues.

The significance of the physical environment must not be overlooked. It is perhaps difficult to believe that the English climate provides good conditions for farming. Winters are rarely long enough to limit crop growth, droughts are rare, and above all rainfall does not vary greatly from year to year. But many Asian and African farmers are constant victims of drought. Where rainfall is low, as it is in much of Africa, total annual rainfall is concentrated in one short part of the year. Not only does the amount received vary greatly from one year to another, but the date at which the rains, and thus the agricultural year, begin is uncertain. In the Indian subcontinent rainfall is, apparently, much greater; but the monsoons are prone to great variations in the amount of rain they bring and in the time they arrive. Below-average monsoons have an obvious effect on harvests but it should not be forgotten that above-average rainfall may cause floods that can destroy harvests in the rivers and deltas where much of India's population lives. . . .

Nearer the Equator, in the humid tropics of the Amazon basin, the Congo basin and the Malaysian archipelago, the growth of the natural vegetation, the tropical rainforest, is so exuberant that it would seem to be the ideal environment for crop growth. Yet outside the lower rivers and deltas, farmers have found it very difficult to crop land continuously. Plant foods constantly move in a nutrient cycle from the soil to the forest. Once the forest has been cleared and crops sown and harvested annually, the soil is exposed to high temperatures and heavy rainfall and it is difficult to prevent a decline in soil fertility. Recent research on potential photosynthesis suggests that the equatorial regions are always likely to support lower yields than the subtropics where there is less cloud and a greater light intensity.

Two changes must take place if these problems are to be overcome. First, a better social and economic framework must be provided for the farmer to work in. Land reform was once thought to be the key to increasing agricultural productivity, endorsing the belief that the farmer who owns his land is more likely to adopt new methods than the farmer who has to give half his harvest to the landlord and much of the rest to the local money-lender. Desirable though land reform may be, it does not necessarily make the farmer a better farmer and many land reform schemes have had disappointing results. Similarly farm size: if farms are too small they should be amalgamated. But what happens to the dispossessed, and the rapidly growing rural populations without land? There are few jobs for them in the towns and far from creating bigger and more efficient farms, many governments have put a limit on sizes of holdings to try to ensure that everyone has some land.

Great hopes were placed on the building of roads and railways. They were expected to shatter the structure of traditional society, drag the farmer into the market place, and encourage efficiency. But once the Afro-Asian farmer finds his way to the world market the prospects are gloomy. Prices for agricultural products are notoriously unstable, and are declining in the long term *vis à vis* the goods that the LDCs [Less Developed Countries] want to buy.

The second part of the problem lies on the farm itself. Most peasant farming systems are efficient, given the environmental and economic conditions within which they have evolved. But to secure the great increases in productivity that are necessary, quite new inputs must be obtained. However, there have been fashions in technological panaceas. Until the early 1960s there was a widespread belief that mechanization, which was the basis of modern agriculture in North America and to a lesser extent in Western Europe, would solve the problem. Only slowly was it realized that the introduction of combine harvesters and caterpillar tractors had little relevance for small farmers.

An intermediate technology which can bridge the gap between the primitive implements of many farmers and the sophisticated machinery of the West is needed. European farmers themselves did not change overnight from sickles and flails to combine harvesters and in the nineteenth century marked advances in productivity were obtained by replacing the sickle with the scythe, and then the scythe with the reaper.

At present, farmers and governments are looking not to labor-saving devices but to methods of obtaining higher yields per hectare. At the center of the green revolution are the new hybrid wheat and rice varieties. Hybrids are obtained by cross-breeding genetically unlike varieties of the same plant, and the aims are higher yields, and more rapid maturity. . . . [But] new technology is essentially capital intensive not labor-intensive, and greatly increased yields can be obtained without using more labor, except where multiple-cropping is adopted. But this does not solve the problems of a rapidly increasing rural population with little hope of jobs in the towns. The new inputs are costly; although yields may triple production, costs rise proportionally and the farmer's outlay must be made before he gets the benefit of greater output.

The new crop varieties have certainly been more revolutionary in their impact than attempts to mechanize Asian agriculture. The threat of famine has receded for the time being but population continues to grow and even the widespread adoption of the new varieties cannot solve the problems of poverty in the rural third world. Long-term increased efficiency must mean fewer people on the land, cheaper and better fertilizers and implements, larger farms and better transport. These will come if industrialization provides jobs for the rural unemployed for this and following generations.

THE NEGEV BLOOMS [5]

The growth and development of Israeli agriculture in the anguished . . . years of its short history almost surpasses the imagination. Having "inherited" sand dunes, thorny scrubland and desert, the Israelis have developed an agriculture which is the fastest growing in the world and is one of the most productive. Amazed at the fantastic feat of transforming the landscape from a harsh barren wilderness into fields and orange groves, no wonder people have got it into their heads that by some miracle of ingenuity and grit the Israelis have made the desert bloom.

Nor is the lie given when traveling south of Beersheba towards the stark moonscape of the Negev with its deep canyons, eroded limestone hills and broad sweeping wadis, etched like wizened wrinkles on the ancient face of the earth; for in that sunscorched emptiness, here and there, one finds the fruits of Israel's labors; a sudden glimpse as one drives down the desert road of a green oasis of cypresses guarding a peach or apricot orchard, or of a battery house for chickens and of cattle grazing out in pasture.

[5] From "Will the Desert Bloom?" by Peter Bunyard, editor, *Ecologist*. *Ecologist*. 3:334-7. S. '73. Reprinted by permission.

But the desert agriculture of Sde Boker and Mashabey Sade, two of the handful of kibbutzim [rural cooperative settlements] that have become established in the driest parts of the Negev, has not been won through some magic use of the very limited rain which falls sharply and briefly during the winter months only to cease for the rest of the year, but through the piping in of water from the Sea of Galilee where rainfall in the wet season is comparatively abundant. Kibbutz Sde Boker obtains only 30 percent of its water from local rain, the rest comes from the Galilee. Kibbutz Mashabey Sade gets as much as one million cubic meters of water each year piped in from Galilee.

Water is the one big limiting factor in Israel and water shortage now threatens to cripple the economy and prevent the rapid industrial expansion and development to which Israelis aspire with something approaching avidity. After the rains have fallen, and most has evaporated or has been transpired through the leaves of plants, the Israelis are left with the water that has drained into the Jordan and the Sea of Galilee as well as with the water that has percolated down to recharge the aquifers along the sandy coastal plain of the Mediterranean and the aquifers to be found in the limestone mountains of the interior. This water, amounting to a maximum of 1,500 million cubic meters each year, has to provide for all Israel's needs, including agriculture, industry and domestic, during the long, dry summer season. The Israelis are now using more than 90 percent of the maximum water available to them and with a couple of dry seasons behind them are facing a very real water shortage indeed. . . .

It is something of a contrast therefore to leave Sde Boker, with its lush green avenue of trees watered unashamedly from a conspicuous irrigation pipe, for [Hebrew University] Professor [Michael] Evenari's experimental farm at Avdat, just a few miles to the south at the edge of the Valley of Zin. Avdat is not lush. When one climbs the hill to reach the ancient and now totally ruined city and looks down at the experimental farm one sees a relatively tiny rectangular patchwork of small fields with widely spaced trees, amid barren wasteland stretching for miles.

Evenari's work and the history of Avdat are intricately interwoven and cannot be separated from each other; for basically what Professor Evenari and his colleagues have done is to reestablish the same system of farming that was developed first by the Nabateans, from the third century BC until the first century AD, and then in its final flourishing by the Byzantines. In the seventh century AD Avdat fell, first to the Persians, and, just a few years later to the Muslims who had no use for the place and left it in ruins. Avdat was rediscovered by an Englishman, E. H. Palmer, in 1871, and it was he who wondered at the innumerable stone mounds and strips that he could see running down the hillside from his vantage point in the ruined city.

Nabatean Agriculture

In essence the system was very simple. The rains in the Negev tend to be heavy and runoff from the hillsides into the wadis soon creates swirling floods that sweep down towards the Rift Valley that divides the great land masses of Asia and Africa. That water, unless checked and directed, is quickly lost, for unlike the other deserts such as the Sinai desert or parts of the Sahara, the Negev desert is very poor in groundwater and the few boreholes that have been made generally produce water too salty for human consumption.

The Nabateans, however, developed an ingenious system of runoff channels, small dams, trenches, terraces and cisterns, whereby they were able to collect water from a wide area and concentrate it all into a single growing area. From rebuilding the water-collecting system at Avdat and to the northwest at Shivta, another Nabatean town that became Byzantine, Evenari estimates that each unit area which was cultivated received water from a catchment area that was twenty to thirty-five times larger.

On average, Avdat and Shivta receive only three to four

inches of rain each year, an amount of rainfall that makes the Negev one of the driest deserts in the world. And being an average it gives no hint of the wide variation that can be expected. In the 1962/63 season Avdat got less than one inch of rain and in the following season six inches. Nevertheless because of the multiplication possible through the use of the runoff system it is quite feasible in an average year to get as much as six thousand cubic meters of water to every hectare of cultivated land—an amount of water equivalent to twenty-four inches of rain.

Inscriptions found at Nizzana, beyond Shivta to the west, show that the Nabateans successfully grew wheat, barley, legumes, almonds and grapes in the desert. Other records left by the Byzantines show that they were able to achieve yields that were remarkably high considering the quantities of water available, and that they did not use modern methods of fertilization and of pest control. Evenari's own results over the past fifteen years on the reconstructed farms give ample, incontestable proof that even in one of the world's harshest deserts it is possible to produce a surplus of food. . . .

Without the watering made possible on the desert kibbutzim by the waters of the Jordan and Galilee, Evenari is unable to get maximum yields from his plants. And some years when the rainfall falls well below average his fruit trees do little more than survive without producing any fruit. Yet on the whole his yields are extraordinarily good considering the conditions in the Negev. Thus over a two-year test period using the ancient farm methods he was able to get 8–12 tons of peaches per hectare, 5–8 tons of apricots, 12–15 tons of grapes, 6–8 tons of figs and 0.43–0.93 tons of dry, shelled almonds.

He also tried pasture crops, testing more than one hundred different species. The most efficient user of water was *Avena sterilis* which gave 2.6 to 2.9 kilograms of dry matter for each cubic meter of water used. Alfalfa also did well, and Evenari obtained 1.8 kg of dry matter for every cubic meter of water even though the total quantities of water received over the year amounted to no more than two thousand cubic meters—equivalent to eight inches of rain. . . .

Because of the success of his negarin the Jerusalem botanist has now begun desert farming on a much bigger scale. Between Mashabey Sade and Beersheba in a hot barren plain close to the Wadi Mashash, Evenari and his colleagues have established a farm based on the negarin principle with some 2,000 almond trees, 500 pistachios and 150 olives. They have also planted 50 hectares of pasture in strips, using the negarin method of runoff to supply the strip with water and are bringing 500 sheep in. The sheep will be watered by runoff collected and piped in from the surrounding hills. . . .

The economics of desert farming seem to be very good. Even with modern machinery the cost of clearing the land and making microcatchments comes to no more than $20 per hectare. . . .

Because of the critical shortage of water in Israel and because of the government's intention to promote industry at the expense of agriculture Professor Evenari's experiments in the desert have taken on a new relevance. Nevertheless many Israeli agronomists shrug off Evenari's work with something approaching irritation, as a kind of clever but crankish exercise in agricultural history but absolutely nothing to do with modern farming and productivity. As one veteran kibbutznik from a desert settlement told me: "The yields obtained at Avdat may be good for nomads and simple farmers, but Europeans cannot work at that low productivity."

In a way what the kibbutznik said is true. The desert cannot be made to bloom using its own resources of water and a European used to high mechanization would find it wasteful and irritating to have to cover large expanses of ground for spraying and fertilizing his crops, and then finding the yields nothing like as good as his neighbors' who can afford to bring water in from outside. Yet the world cannot afford to do what the Israelis have done and for the simple man in Afghan or in the Sahara Evenari's experiments may be the one hope that they have left.

FISH FARMING [6]

Reprinted from *U.S. News & World Report*.

After struggling along for years as a "back yard" industry, fish farming is starting to take off as a promising business in America.

The trend for some markets already is well established.

Most of the trout available in the grocery freezer today, for example, does not come from the sparkling waters of a mountain stream. It is methodically bred, fed, harvested and packaged on huge trout farms in the West and South.

An estimated 95 percent of the catfish sold in the United States—a market worth more than $30 million annually—comes from aquacultural enterprises ranging from small ponds on family farms to the elaborate fish-farming complexes valued at hundreds of thousands of dollars.

Big Names

Another tip-off to the growing importance of fish farming is the swelling list of big company names that are getting involved in research and, to some extent, marketing. The list includes: Ralston Purina, United Brands, Armour, Florida Power & Light, General Mills, Long Island Lighting Company and Pacific Gas & Electric.

The utilities on the list are discovering that the water they use to cool power plants can make an excellent warm-water environment for accelerated fish growth.

A recent report by Frost & Sullivan, Inc., a New York–based research firm, forecasts a "dynamic expansion" of fish farming in the United States from today's level of $54 million to $374 million by 1982.

The National Marine Fisheries Service reports that 143

[6] From "Fish Farming—It's Catching On." *U.S. News & World Report*. 78:74. Ap. 21, '75.

million pounds of sea food was grown in captivity in 1973—the last year for which figures are available. Catfish and trout accounted for 60 percent of the production, with salmon, oysters, crayfish, clams and shrimp making up most of the rest.

Most trout and catfish are grown in fresh water, which is called "aquaculture." The production of salt-water species is called "mariculture."

The growing interest in fish farming comes at a time when the world catch on the high seas is erratic. There are not enough of some prime species to satisfy climbing global demand.

No. 1 Producer: Japan

One obvious answer to the rising supply-and-demand squeeze is to grow sea food in a controlled environment. This is being done in many parts of the world. One illustration is Japan. It is recognized as the world's leading producer, and annually harvests more than 450,000 tons from its fish farms—about 6 percent of all sea food sold in Japan.

One species that experts say has the richest potential for fish farming is the shrimp. It grows rapidly—allowing several harvests per year—demand is worldwide, and the price is high. No other species is receiving as much attention from the research community. . . .

Other research programs are striving to start or to increase production of mariculture crabs, lobsters, oysters, clams, salmon, scallops, abalone and mullet.

One of the biggest problems faced by this enterprise is lack of control over coastal waters. Because of strict coast-line-development legislation, says one entrepreneur, it is difficult for commercial fish farmers to set up an operation along beaches or in shallow water as is done in other countries. This factor will have a dramatic influence on the economics of fish farming in the U.S.

Double Goal

Another aspect of mariculture research is being explored at Woods Hole Oceanographic Institution in Massachusetts. John Ryther, a marine biologist, is growing oysters, seaweed and sometimes flounder in tanks fed by a constant stream of partially treated sewage. His goal is both to clean up the sewage and to grow marine life that is competitive on a commercial market.

He starts the process by pumping a mixture of sewage and sea water into an open pond. When the pond turns green with a bloom of algae, he feeds the nutrient-rich soup into tanks filled with racks of oysters. The oysters gorge themselves on algae. Droppings from the oysters cover the tank bottom providing fertile ground for prolific sea-worm growth—a favorite in the diet of the bottom-feeding flounder.

Finally, water is passed through one additional tank where commercially valuable seaweed is grown. Each step in the process cleans the water and provides food for accelerated growth of marine organisms.

Mr. Ryther says there are still many problems to be worked out in his experiment, but he is optimistic that a system similar to his will one day be both treating sewage and providing food for the dining-room table.

As for the overall potential of aquaculture and mariculture, most observers point out that the industry is still in its infancy.

Ross Clouston, head of the National Fisheries Institute and an executive with a General Mills subsidiary, says:

"Expectations are high for the future of fish farming. The technology upon which this industry will be based is being developed right now."

NEW EMPHASIS ON RESEARCH [7]

In its closing days [in 1974] the 93d Congress made a major shift in American food policy toward the only real answer to world food problems—*increasing food production in developing countries.*

The Foreign Aid bill authorized one half billion dollars for 1975 for technical assistance in food and nutrition programs administered by the Agency for International Development (AID) in the State Department. When actual appropriations are added to repaid loan funds already available, AID officials expect to have almost two thirds billion dollars to spend on food and nutrition activities in developing countries—double the amount spent in recent years.

This impressive boost in research and technology in food and agriculture for developing countries doesn't affect food *aid*—grain shipments—made through USDA's PL 480 program. This is expected to total around $1 billion this year.

However, Congress amended the Foreign Aid bill *to specify that 70 percent of PL 480 food aid must go to the most seriously needy* countries. This is new. Previous Administrations have been accused of directing most food aid to political allies such as Vietnam.

Will this new emphasis on research really work? The potential is there:

"We've reached the point where, for the first time, we can manage the world food problem—if only we will," Sterling Wortman, vice president of the Rockefeller Foundation, told newsmen. . . . He echoes Secretary of State Kissinger at the World Food Conference: "The profound promise of our era is that, for the first time, we may have the technical capacity to free mankind from hunger."

Wortman, and others like him on the staffs of the Rockefeller and Ford foundations, back their opinions with successful experience. The American foundations supported

[7] From "The Real Answer to Starvation," by Roe C. Black, executive editor of *Farm Journal. Farm Journal.* 99:32-3+. F. '75. Reprinted by permission.

the work at the first international research institutes in
Mexico and the Philippines, which produced the miracle
wheat and rice of the green revolution. But they're realists,
too. They know (1) the problem of assembling *all* of the
inputs necessary for high rates of production, including fertilizer, water, new management methods, credit and more;
and (2) the discouragements in efforts to stem the population explosion.

Still, there is hope. Says Wortman: "We have the agricultural research framework set up to attack the problems of
increasing production. We have an unprecedented ability
to marshal research funds on an international scale for
increasing production and delivering the results to the
farmer."

Most of the world still hasn't geared up, even though
we've had extensive agricultural research programs in the
United States for almost one hundred years. Until its feeble
start in the mid-fifties, research on *food crops* basic in the
subtropical and tropical world was virtually nonexistent.
What research there was concentrated on export crops like
bananas, rubber and coffee.

But that's changing fast. Today, many test stations and
scientific projects are underway. Among the most promising
are the eight "international" research institutes—The International:

☐ Rice Research Institute (IRRI), one of the two oldest
centers where miracle rice was developed [See "San Bartolome and the Green Revolution," in this section, above.]

☐ Maize and Wheat Improvement Center (CIMMYT)
in Mexico, where Nobel prize winner Norman Borlaug continues work on those grains [See "Borlaug and the Green
Revolution," in this section, above.]

☐ Institute of Tropical Agriculture (IITA) in Nigeria,
focusing on farming systems for the humid tropics and use
of tropical soils

☐ Center of Tropical Agriculture (CIAT) in Colombia, a pioneer in effective farming systems for lowland tropical areas of the Western Hemisphere

☐ Crops Research Institute for the Semi-Arid Tropics (ICRISAT), in India, which emphasizes farming systems and water conservation methods of benefit to small farmers in hot, water-short regions

☐ Potato Center (CIP) in Peru, a one-crop institute working to expand potato cultivation in developing regions

☐ Laboratory for Research on Animal Diseases (ILRAD) in Kenya, one of the newest centers currently concentrating on immunological methods for controlling East Coast fever and sleeping sickness

☐ Livestock Center for Africa (ILCA) to be located in Ethiopia

The goals of these centers are not idle dreams. The miracle wheat and rice varieties developed in the sixties doubled production in many areas of Asia and Latin America, when accompanied by related practices.

We now know, too, that peasant farmers will adopt new seeds and farming methods as rapidly as American farmers, when given a chance. In just six years, millions of farmers over an area as large as the winter wheat area of the United States adopted the new seeds and new methods of the green revolution. That's faster than hybrid corn was accepted by American farmers in the thirties.

The need to double world food production is urgent. World population is going to double by the year 2000, at the present rate of growth.

The immediate challenge is to increase production on land already in cultivation. Developing countries increased grain yields by only 32 percent over the past twenty years, while developed countries boosted yields by 63 percent. But better seeds and more fertilizer are only part of the answer. For example, a very large number of irrigation systems already in existence in developing countries are operating at less than 50 percent efficiency, a United Nations study shows.

Renovation of about half of existing world irrigation facilities might be feasible between now and 1985, says the United Nations study. Costs: around $21 billion.

Fertilizer supply and distribution is another place we can put on the heat. "Even with high prices, world fertilizer supplies have reached a volume which allows broad fertilizer use on the world's food crops," says Sterling Wortman. Huge new amounts of fertilizer could be available in a few years if the Arabs would develop the great tonnage of natural gas flared off in their Mideast oil fields today.

In four huge regions of the globe, especially, the potential is tremendous. They're in the same dormant state that our Great Plains was 125 years ago when the first western explorers dubbed it "The Great American Desert." Greatest of all is the Amazon Basin in Brazil, followed by the Mekong Delta in South Vietnam and Cambodia, the southern Sudan with only 9 percent of its arable land now in cultivation and the savannah grasslands of Africa. Experts say it would take $1 billion and ten years of work to eradicate sleeping sickness in the African grassland. But when completed, the area would support 120 million head of cattle, almost as many as there are in the United States today.

Considering the antianimal agriculture propaganda at the United Nations World Food Conference [WFC], it may seem strange to find UN studies proposing the development of livestock industries. But it's only strange if you consider it anything but "propaganda." A study prepared by UN economists and scientists months before the WFC in Rome says: "The future of nutritional improvement depends in no small degree on a successful modernization of the developing countries' livestock and fish industries." And "Animal husbandry can play a vital role in improving both the income of the small farmer and diet of his family."

Assuming that it is possible to lick the world food problem technically, the question still is—will we?

Secretary of Agriculture Earl Butz, normally an exuberant optimist about what farmers can do given the tools, is not so optimistic about this one. He says that there are two parts of the world food equation—increasing food production and slowing population growth. "To falter in either, or to fail at either, is to court disaster," the Secretary said.

After the third world contemptuously rejected any talk of population control at UN conferences at Bucharest and Rome . . . [in 1974], there's reason for discouragement. We only have to look across the border for a horrible example. Fifteen years of dramatic advances in wheat production made Mexico a net exporter of cereals by the late sixties. But its population explosion, one of the greatest in the world, has made Mexico a net food importer again.

International cooperation in many areas is far from assured, though agricultural research seems to be a bright spot.

Financing for the international research institutes listed in this article is now being furnished by twenty-nine governments, agencies and foundations. And the funding is rising dramatically from $15 million in 1972, to $23 million in 1973 and $45 million in 1975. And more help is promised. Secretary Kissinger told the WFC:

"We propose that resources for the eight international research centers be more than doubled by 1980. For its part, the United States will, in that same period, triple its own contribution for the international centers, for agricultural research efforts in the less developed countries by American universities."

Recent actions of the Congress are a good start on fulfilling this commitment.

IV. FOOD SUPPLY VS. POPULATION: A SOLVABLE RIDDLE?

EDITOR'S INTRODUCTION

The earth has often been likened to a spaceship, with limited accommodations for crew and passengers. In another analogy, we Americans (or we Africans or we Asians) live in a lifeboat, which will sink if too many people get in. More food supports more people who in turn require more food.

These are conclusions set forth in one form or another by theoreticians and experts for nearly two centuries. Are these dire statements valid? Can we solve the riddle of expanding food supply versus expanding numbers of the earth's inhabitants? Is the problem itself more phantom than reality?

As the eighteenth century came to a close, the English clergyman economist Thomas Malthus set forth his theory of population and food supply, an excerpt of which introduces this section. His theory, cast aside until recently as overly pessimistic, is now being seriously reconsidered. A related view was offered in 1968 by C. P. Snow, the noted author and scientist, in his much quoted Westminster College lecture, a portion of which is included in this section. More recently, the president of the National Academy of Sciences, Dr. Philip Handler, added his thoughts on the need for population control as the essential course to insure sufficient food for all. Then articles by Garrett Hardin and by Norman Cousins debate the current "lifeboat" theory.

Finally, a writer on world food supply, Frances Moore Lappe, takes the view that it is not the absolute quantity of food which is our problem, but its balanced distribution. All commentators agree, however, that the world food crisis and the number of mouths to be fed are clearly interrelated.

THE MALTHUSIAN THEORY [1]

I think I may fairly make two postulata.

First, That food is necessary to the existence of man.

Secondly, That the passion between the sexes is necessary and will remain nearly in its present state.

These two laws, ever since we have had any knowledge of mankind, appear to have been fixed laws of our nature, and, as we have not hitherto seen any alteration in them, we have no right to conclude that they will ever cease to be what they now are, without an immediate act of power in that Being who first arranged the system of the universe, and for the advantage of his creatures, still executes, according to fixed laws, all its various operations.

I do not know that any writer has supposed that on this earth man will ultimately be able to live without food. But Mr. Godwin has conjectured that the passion between the sexes may in time be extinguished. As, however, he calls this part of his work a deviation into the land of conjecture, I will not dwell longer upon it at present than to say that the best arguments for the perfectibility of man are drawn from a contemplation of the great progress that has already [been] made from the savage state and the difficulty of saying where he is to stop. But towards the extinction of the passion between the sexes, no progress whatever has hitherto been made. It appears to exist in as much force at present as it did two thousand or four thousand years ago. There are individual exceptions now as there always have been. But, as these exceptions do not appear to increase in number, it would surely be a very unphilosophical mode of arguing, to infer merely from the existence of an exception, that the exception would, in time, become the rule, and the rule the exception.

Assuming then, my postulata as granted, I say, that the

[1] From *On Population* (First Essay, 1798), by Thomas Robert Malthus, English economist. Text from Modern Library edition, ed. and introd. by Gertrude Himmelfarb. Random House. '60. p 8-9.

power of population is indefinitely greater than the power
in the earth to produce subsistence for man.

Population, when unchecked, increases in a geometrical
ratio. Subsistence increases only in an arithmetical ratio. A
slight acquaintance with numbers will shew the immensity
of the first power in comparison of the second.

By that law of our nature which makes food necessary
to the life of man, the effects of these two unequal powers
must be kept equal.

This implies a strong and constantly operating check on
population from the difficulty of subsistence. This difficulty
must fall somewhere and must necessarily be severely felt by
a large portion of mankind.

THE MOST IMPORTANT QUESTIONS [2]

Unfortunately, there are nearly twice as many people in
the poor countries as in the rich. Further, there will—nothing can stop it—be an extra billion people added to the
world population in the next ten years. Of those, rather
more than three quarters will be added to the poor. All
these statements . . . are clichés. A lot of us—and most urgently of all, American demographers and food scientists—
have been uttering them for years past. Here is another. The
gap between the rich and poor countries is growing. Take
the average daily income in a large slice of the poor countries. . . . [In 1968 it was] something like $.35 a day. The
average daily income in the United States . . . [was] about
$8 a day. Twenty times greater. In ten years it is likely to be
thirty times greater.

Yes, those statements are clichés, all right. Some of them
are dreadful clichés: and I am using dreadful in its first
meaning, that is full of dread. The most dreadful of all—

[2] From *The State of Siege*, the 1968 John Findley Green Foundation Lecture
delivered at Westminster College, Fulton, Missouri, by C. P. Snow, Baron Snow,
British author and former government official and adviser. Scribner. '71. p 23-31.
Excerpt is reprinted by permission of Charles Scribner's Sons. Copyright © 1969
C. P. Snow.

again, men of sober judgment have been saying it for years —is that many millions of people in the poor countries are going to starve to death before our eyes—or, to complete the domestic picture, we shall see them doing so upon our television sets.

How soon? How many deaths? Can they be prevented? Can they be minimized?

Those are the most important questions in our world today. Much more important than all the things which fret us in Western societies—student power, racial conflicts, the disaffection of the young. Though I believe there is an invisible connection between our local problems and the catastrophic world one.

To answer those questions we have to rely to an extent upon judgment—which is really informed guessing. Most of the expert demographers and the agronomists take the most pessimistic view. It is usually right, in matters of judgment, to take a pessimistic view—so long as it doesn't inhibit one totally from action, even inadequate action. That is a lesson which we have all learned who have had any experience of war. But I want to stress that neither the extent of this catastrophe, nor the time it will happen, nor whether it will go on indefinitely or be controlled, can be precisely calculated. There are too many unknowns. One of the unknowns, or half-knowns, gives a glimmer of partial hope. I shall deal with that shortly. The only contribution I can make is to give my own judgment, for what it is worth. It is worth only as much or as little as anyone else's who can read the evidence. I am neither a demographer nor an agronomist. And there are different stresses of opinion among those who know most, and some areas of disagreement.

It is common ground that in large parts of the poor world, in sections of Asia, Africa, Latin America, the collision between rising population and available food is very near. The demographers say that there is no method of curtailing the rate of population-growth within ten years.

With great good fortune, and world effort, a little might just conceivably be done in twenty or thirty years. They call on the agronomists to pull something out of the bag to give the demographers enough time. The agronomists—or a large proportion of them—make exactly the same demand in reverse. Can the demographers reduce the human increase soon enough to give *them*—the people working on tropical agriculture—enough time?

Most informed opinion believes that neither step is going to happen in time: that is, the collision is going to take place. At best, this will mean local famines to begin with. At worst, the local famines will spread into a sea of hunger. The usual date predicted for the beginning of the local famines is 1975–80, though I believe that may be over-pessimistic.

The only rational ground for putting this date further into the future is the hope of increasing food production. In fact, this is the chief area of disagreement between responsible men. Here, as it happens, there is the glimmer, the ray of hope, that I mentioned. In the midst of the bleak prospect, there is one genuine piece—though in the long term it mustn't be over-estimated—of good news. . . .

[The author here comments on achievements in India, Pakistan, and the Philippines toward sharply increased wheat and rice production.—Ed.]

Well, this is good news. In making one's judgment of the future, it is a factor. We mustn't lose our heads, one way or the other. The limits to food production, even when as deeply planned as this, seem to be quite sharp. The population increase has no such limits. The collision is still on. The guess I should now make—as I said, this is no more useful than that of anyone else who reads the evidence—is that large-scale famine won't happen as early as 1975–80. There will probably (it is a bitter thing to say) be serious local famines, in, for instance, Latin America and parts of Africa. The major catastrophe will happen before the end of the century. We shall, in the rich countries, be surrounded by a sea of famine, involving hundreds of millions of human beings unless three tremendous social tasks are by then in operation. Not just one alone, but all three. They are:

1. a concerted effort by the rich countries to produce food, money and technical assistance for the poor
2. an effort by the poor countries themselves, on the lines of India and Pakistan, to revolutionize their food production
3. an effort by the poor countries—with all the assistance that can be provided under (1)—to reduce or stop their population increase: with a corresponding reduction in the population increase in the rich countries too

Those are the three conditions, all necessary, if we are to avoid social despair.

THE STATE OF MAN [3]

Worldwide disaster may be possible within the lifetimes of persons already born. Denial that the relatively near future could witness large-scale disaster rests, it seems to me, more on optimistic articles of faith than on scientific analysis. The prospects of an imminent world food shortage, and of a not distant day when the supply of fossil fuels and other critical minerals will be insufficient to support the world economy seem to me to be virtually self-evident.

Let it be clear that the growth of human populations is the principal and most compelling threat to the survival of the species. All other aspects of human behavior are secondary. The annual growth rate of the human population, expressed as a percentage of the base, remained very low for almost all of the few million years since the first Homo sapiens trod the planet. Had we started with but one pair, the present population could have been attained by about

[3] From article by Dr. Philip Handler, president, National Academy of Sciences. *War on Hunger.* 9:1-4+. F. '75.

30 consecutive doublings, which need only have taken one millennium. In actuality, it is estimated that the annual population growth rate worldwide was of the order of 0.02 percent until only a few centuries ago. That growth rate, which began to rise noticeably during the eighteenth century and increased sharply during the nineteenth century, became startling only within our own life times. For the planet as a whole that rate is now about 2 percent annually, being as high as 3.5 percent in some countries and zero or even negative in only a few.

Most of the developed countries have gone through what is called the "demographic transition." When industrialization began, in parallel, as a result of a relatively assured food supply and the introduction of only modest hygienic and sanitation measures, there was a precipitate decline in the mortality rate, largely of infants and very young children, with no decline in fertility for some while. During that period, populations in Europe, the United States and Japan grew rapidly; since then the fertility rate has declined to virtually match the death rate and the populations of these countries are on the way to population stabilization.

Colonialism's Mixed Blessings

But the rest of the world was under the yoke of colonialism—for which it must pay a fearful price that no one foresaw. To huge geographic areas the Western masters brought those same hygienic measures which were effective in their own countries, while failing to encourage the development of local industry. In so doing, they brought down the mortality rate in varying degree, but failed to initiate that economic development which by providing jobs, income, health care, literacy, better diets, and improving the status of women, also generates the incentives and motivation for the spontaneous decline in fertility that accompanied development in Europe, the United States and Japan. And so these populations grew—and grew.

The large mass of the developing world has yet to go through the demographic transition and, in consequence, the human population now at four billion, is driving toward six to seven billion at the turn of the century. It is unlikely to stabilize before world population is above ten or twelve billion, unless other phenomena intervene—as well they may. *Stated most simply, if mankind is to live in the state of material well-being that technology can make possible, then given the finite size and resources of the planet, there are just too many of us already, and no additions should be welcome.* If today, all mankind were to experience the material standard of living of the United States—in a general way, the rate of extraction of the critical minerals in the earth's crust would have to increase by a factor of 17. Given the developing shortages of many of these materials even now, that is patently impossible.

Consequences of Population Growth

Some years ago, in a book entitled *Biology and the Future of Man,* I wrote:

Many of the most tragic ills of human existence find their origin in population growth—hunger, pollution, crime, despoliation of the natural beauty of the planet, irreversible extermination of countless species of plants and animals, overlarge, dirty, overcrowded cities with their paradoxical loneliness, continual erosion of limited natural resources and the seething unrest which creates the political instability that leads to international conflict and war, all derive from the unbridled growth of human populations. . . . As population growth continues, inevitably there will be instances in which the food supply to one or another region will become, even if temporarily, grossly inadequate and on so large a scale that organized world food relief will be woefully incommensurate. And the resultant political instability could have gigantic consequences for all mankind.

Is that day in sight? Let us look first to the near future, to the fact that world food reserves have dropped from an 80-day to a 20-day supply in only a few years. North America is now the only region of the world that produces significantly more than it can consume, exporting a "surplus" equivalent to about 8 percent of total world grain production. Predictions abound of starvation on such scale that more people will starve to death in the twentieth century than in any other century in the history of man. It is estimated that there were about 2 million such deaths in the seventeenth century, 10 million in the eighteenth century, and perhaps 25 million in the nineteenth century. Despite the world's information network, the remarkable worldwide transportation system, and the prolific yields of modern agriculture—where modern agriculture is practiced—available indications suggest that the death toll due to starvation in this century, indeed in the next few years, will set an all-time high. More people may starve to death simply because there are more people.

Worldwide, annual primary food production, now about 1,200 million tons of cereal grain, has continued to grow more rapidly than has the total human population, roughly 2.5 percent per year as against 2 percent. But the great increases in production have not occurred where the population is growing most rapidly. The great gains in cereal production have occurred where modern energy intensive agriculture—as developed in the United States, largely with federal research support—has combined applied genetics, irrigation, pesticides and herbicides, fertilizer and mechanization to the increase of yields. . . .

Even now there are perhaps 400 million individuals whose lives are limited by the quality of their diets. As populations grow, that company will surely expand. For them, life is a succession of diseases and an apathetic struggle for bare survival. It is noteworthy that the character of malnutrition has changed markedly in the last forty to fifty years. The classical deficiency diseases—beri beri, scurvy, pellagra, rickets, sprue—have almost disappeared. Of those, only xerophthalmia due to Vitamin A deficiency continues as a serious problem, causing blindness in large numbers of children. Instead, there is marasmus, and kwashiorkor—both

forms of general protein-calorie insufficiency, i.e., semi-star-
vation, and iron deficiency anemia. *Thus, nutritional status
is now rarely the consequence of ignorance; malnutrition
now reflects lack of food, not lack of scientific understanding. . . .*

Building Reserves, Limiting Consumption

The often discussed concept of a "world food bank,"
really a "world grain bank," is clearly the principal device
by which it would be possible to mitigate the duress of crop
failure in any part of the world. Patently, North America
must serve as the principal source of the grain in that bank.
Were gross world production in any year truly in excess of
potential demand, the reserve could be accumulated readily,
an analogy with the history of the US reserve which was
the excess of American production over consumption. But
on a global scale, the analogy fails in some part since bil-
lions would like to eat better than their incomes now make
possible. The world grain bank can only be accumulated if
it is done by a formula in which the peoples of developed
nations impose self-restraint on their own consumption—by
whatever device they choose—and if all affluent nations join
the taxpayers of the United States in purchasing from the
farmers of North America the grain that they produce. Re-
alistically, under current circumstances that means that the
oil exporting nations must make a major contribution to
this scheme. Sales from the bank to developing nations with
acute food shortages must then be made at well below cost.
Agreement to an equitable formula by which this can be
achieved is a difficult but imperative international task. By
1985, the developing countries will require about 85 million
tons of imported grain per year, an amount that surely can
be made available if there is gathered the political will to
pay for it.

What of the longer term future of food supplies? It is
extremely dubious that even markedly enhanced agricultural productivity will keep pace with population growth

unless there is a very early and marked decrease in the rate of growth of the populations of the developing nations.

Indeed, if the peoples of the developing nations are to know a standard of living which would be deemed acceptable in our eyes, primary agricultural production in those countries must grow significantly more rapidly than does population. That seems distinctly possible everywhere except in South Asia. The population is already immense—about 850 million—and growing at about 2.5 percent per year, with a birthrate of about 45 per thousand. It seems utterly unlikely that that birthrate can be brought down before the turn of the century to a level which will permit subsequent attainment of equilibrium. By that time the population of South Asia could be twice what it is at present. To be sure, equilibrium is inevitable. But whereas in the developed world equilibrium will entail a low birthrate and long mean life span, in South Asia and perhaps elsewhere, it now seems that equilibrium may mean a high birthrate and short mean life span.

Without unprecedented, massive external food assistance, therefore, one must anticipate millions of child deaths annually in South Asia alone in the next two decades and tens of millions of such deaths thereafter. There seems little chance of the accumulation of sufficient capital in these nations for their industrialization or for the development of their own agricultural enterprise on a scale commensurate with need in the relatively near future if they must rely on their own resources. Unless there is an abrupt decline in their fertility, the food aid that will be required will soon equal our entire American food surplus. Early in the next century they could require assistance equal to our entire agricultural production.

The question is not whether the arable land of the planet, appropriately managed, could reasonably feed a significantly larger population than at present. Undoubtedly it could. The question is whether the multiplicity of resources required will be gathered and brought to bear within the countries of the "Fourth World," particularly South Asia, in sufficient time and amount to provide the infrastructure, education and resources necessary to increase agricultural production while also increasing real per capita income. Decline in fertility, rather than an increase in the death rate, might then become the brake on the growth of human population before the physical limitations of the planet do become the limiting condition for the size of the human population.

It seems imperative that the situation in the "Fourth World" be understood as thoroughly as possible by our policy makers, those of the other developed nations, and those who control the accumulating capital of the oil exporting nations. For the present, their plight can be alleviated only by food aid, as required. But, for the longer term, the decision must be either to make a truly all-out effort to assist those areas to attain self-sufficiency or to abstain. A partial effort, such as minimal food aid, alone, is probably intrinsically counterproductive. Assistance which barely manages to keep people alive and hungry and without hope leaves them in just the state in which there is no incentive for family planning, thereby feeding population growth rather than checking it. A food crisis among a billion people would then be alleviated only so that the world would later confront a food crisis on a yet larger scale. Cruel as it may sound, if the affluent nations do not intend the colossal total effort commensurate with this task, it may then be wiser to "let nature take its course." . . .

Thus, there appears no acceptable alternative to the imperative of a worldwide political commitment to the abatement of population growth. That was not accomplished at the [UN population] meeting at Bucharest in 1974. One can, however, take solace from the very fact that such a meeting did occur. We can hope that at subsequent meetings there will be more willingness to address the brutal reality of these problems. It is true, as some nations argued at Bucharest, that in the now developed world the demographic transition spontaneously followed the process of development and occurred when the standard of living became sufficiently high, education, medical care, nutrition and employment were virtually assured, and the status of women improved. But if we must repeat that same sequence in the developing nations, *because those nations start with already large population bases* their ultimate populations will be of horrendous magnitude and the quality of life inversely proportional. If there is not sufficient food, then a steady increase in some national death rates will become inevitable. Accordingly, one cannot wait for a spontaneous demographic transition. While agricultural and industrial development are assisted and food aid provided, an aggressive worldwide population policy is imperative.

Change in Life Style Inevitable

Thus, there falls upon the industrialized world, particularly upon the United States, and upon the oil exporting nations, the burden to provide capital and technical assistance to the peoples of the developing nations so as to enable most, if not all of them, one day to feed themselves. But such assistance must be paralleled by corresponding national political commitments to population control. Given the physical limitations of the planet, however well we do, a drastic change is inevitable in the life style of those privileged to live in the most developed nations.

Successful, intensive agriculture is a research intensive enterprise and each developing nation must be enabled to manage its agricultural research for itself. And again, the burden is upon scientists to assist them in learning the rudiments of this function. At the same time, the principal burden for the performance of the relevant fundamental research certainly falls upon us.

The fruits of science did much to make our civilization worthwhile; now only political leadership combined with yet more science can save that civilization. Withal, the quality of life for our descendants will be determined primarily by how many of them there will be.

LIVING ON A LIFEBOAT [4]

Approximately two thirds of the world is desperately poor, and only one third is comparatively rich. The people in poor countries have an average per capita GNP (Gross National Product) of about $200 per year; the rich, of about $3,000. (For the United States it is nearly $5,000 per year.) Metaphorically, each rich nation amounts to a lifeboat full of comparatively rich people. The poor of the world are in other, much more crowded lifeboats. Continuously, so to speak, the poor fall out of their lifeboats and swim for a while in the water outside, hoping to be admitted to a rich lifeboat, or in some other way to benefit from the "goodies" on board. What should the passengers on a rich lifeboat do? This is the central problem of "the ethics of a lifeboat."

First we must acknowledge that each lifeboat is effectively limited in capacity. The land of every nation has a limited carrying capacity. The exact limit is a matter for argument, but the energy crunch is convincing more people every day that we have already exceeded the carrying capacity of the land. We have been living on "capital"—stored petroleum and coal—and soon we must live on income alone.

Let us look at only one lifeboat—ours. The ethical problem is the same for all, and is as follows. Here we sit, say 50 people in a lifeboat. To be generous, let us assume our boat has a capacity of 10 more, making 60. (This, however, is to violate the engineering principle of the "safety factor." A new plant disease or a bad change in the weather may

[4] From article by Garrett Hardin, professor of human ecology, University of California at Santa Barbara. *BioScience.* 24:561-8. O. '74. Reprinted, with permission, from the October 1974 issue of *BioScience* published by the American Institute of Biological Sciences.

decimate our population if we don't preserve some excess capacity as a safety factor.)

The 50 of us in the lifeboat see 100 others swimming in the water outside, asking for admission to the boat, or for handouts. How shall we respond to their calls? There are several possibilities.

One. We may be tempted to try to live by the Christian ideal of being "our brother's keeper," or by the Marxian ideal (Marx 1875) of "from each according to his abilities, to each according to his needs." Since the needs of all are the same, we take all the needy into our boat, making a total of 150 in a boat with a capacity of 60. The boat is swamped, and everyone drowns. Complete justice, complete catastrophe.

Two. Since the boat has an unused excess capacity of 10, we admit just 10 more to it. This has the disadvantage of getting rid of the safety factor, for which action we will sooner or later pay dearly. Moreover, *which* 10 do we let in? "First come, first served?" The best 10? The neediest 10? How do we *discriminate?* And what do we say to the 90 who are excluded?

Three. Admit no more to the boat and preserve the small safety factor. Survival of the people in the lifeboat is then possible (though we shall have to be on our guard against boarding parties).

The last solution is abhorrent to many people. It is unjust, they say. Let us grant that it is.

"I feel guilty about my good luck," say some. The reply to this is simple: *Get out and yield your place to others.* Such a selfless action might satisfy the conscience of those who are addicted to guilt but it would not change the ethics of the lifeboat. The needy person to whom a guilt-addict yields his place will not himself feel guilty about his sudden good luck. (If he did he would not climb aboard.) The net result of conscience-stricken people relinquishing their unjustly held positions is the elimination of their kind of conscience from the lifeboat. The lifeboat, as it were, purifies itself of guilt. The ethics of the lifeboat persist, unchanged by such momentary aberrations.

This then is the basic metaphor within which we must work out our solutions. Let us enrich the image step by step with substantive additions from the real world.

Reproduction

The harsh characteristics of lifeboat ethics are heightened by reproduction, particularly by reproductive differences. The people inside the lifeboats of the wealthy nations are doubling in numbers every 87 years; those outside are doubling every 35 years, on the average. And the relative difference in prosperity is becoming greater.

Let us, for a while, think primarily of the US lifeboat. As of 1973 the United States had a population of 210 million people, who were increasing by 0.8 percent per year, that is, doubling in number every 87 years.

Although the citizens of rich nations are outnumbered two to one by the poor, let us imagine an equal number of poor people outside our lifeboat—a mere 210 million poor people reproducing at a quite different rate. If we imagine these to be the combined populations of Colombia, Venezuela, Ecuador, Morocco, Thailand, Pakistan, and the Philippines, the average rate of increase of people "outside" is 3.3 percent per year. The doubling time of this population is 21 years.

Suppose that all these countries, and the United States, agreed to live by the Marxian ideal, "to each according to his needs," the ideal of most Christians as well. Needs, of course, are determined by population size, which is affected by reproduction. Every nation regards its rate of reproduction as a sovereign right. If our lifeboat were big enough in the beginning it might be possible to live *for a while* by Christian-Marxian ideals. *Might.*

Initially, in the model given, the ratio of non-Americans to Americans would be one to one. But consider what the ratio would be 87 years later. By this time Americans would have doubled to a population of 420 million. The other group (doubling every 21 years) would now have swollen to 3,540 million. Each American would have more than eight people to share with. How could the lifeboat possibly keep afloat?

All this involves extrapolation of current trends into the future, and is consequently suspect. Trends may change. Granted: but the change will not necessarily be favorable. If—as seems likely—the rate of population increase falls faster in the ethnic group presently inside the lifeboat than it does among those now outside, the future will turn out to be even worse than mathematics predicts, and sharing will be even more suicidal.

Ruin in the Commons

The fundamental error of the sharing ethics is that it leads to the tragedy of the commons. Under a system of private property the man (or group of men) who own property recognize their responsibility to care for it, for if they don't they will eventually suffer. A farmer, for instance, if he is intelligent, will allow no more cattle in a pasture than its carrying capacity justifies. If he overloads the pasture, weeds take over, erosion sets in, and the owner loses in the long run.

But if a pasture is run as a commons open to all, the right of each to use it is not matched by an operational responsibility to take care of it. It is no use asking independent herdsmen in a commons to act responsibly, for they dare not. The considerate herdsman who refrains from overloading the commons suffers more than a selfish one who says his needs are greater. (As Leo Durocher says, "Nice guys finish last.") Christian-Marxian idealism is counterproductive. That it *sounds* nice is no excuse. With distribution systems, as with individual morality, good intentions are no substitute for good performance.

A social system is stable only if it is insensitive to errors. To the Christian-Marxian idealist a selfish person is a sort of "error." Prosperity in the system of the commons cannot survive errors. If *everyone* would only restrain himself, all would be well; but it takes *only one less than everyone* to ruin a system of voluntary restraint. In a crowded world of less than perfect human beings—and we will never know any other—mutual ruin is inevitable in the commons. This is the core of the tragedy of the commons.

OF LIFE AND LIFEBOATS [5]

A short distance outside New Delhi, I saw a long file of protest marchers walking slowly in the direction of the capital. Most of them were young adults. They were identified by their placards as teachers, students, farmers, shopkeepers, commercial workers.

One of the placards said: HUNGRY PEOPLE ARE HUMAN, TOO. Another sign: IS INDIA GOING TO BE THROWN ON THE RUBBISH HEAP?

I learned that the reason for the march was the increasing discussion in the Indian press over reports that Western nations, including the United States, are getting ready to turn their backs on India's starving millions. The reports suggest that Western policy-makers feel that no amount of aid can prevent mass famine.

A person whose name has been linked frequently to such a hard-line approach is Garrett Hardin, professor of biology at the University of California, Santa Barbara. According to the reports, Professor Hardin believes that the Western nations are justified in denying aid to famine-threatened countries. He uses the analogy of the lifeboat. If the survivors take more than a certain number on board, everyone will go down.

Professor Hardin's ideas and the shocked reaction of the young people on the New Delhi march serve to dramatize what is rapidly becoming the most important issue before

[5] Editorial by Norman Cousins, editor, *Saturday Review*. *Saturday Review*. 2:4. Mr. 8, '75. Reprinted by permission.

contemporary civilization. The attitudes of the rich toward
the poor and the poor toward the rich are setting the stage
for what could become the costliest showdown in history.
C. P. Snow sees a world divided between the 75 percent who
are starving and the 25 percent who are sitting in their living rooms watching it happen on TV. [See "The Most Important Questions," in this section, above.] Robert Heilbroner, in *An Inquiry Into the Human Prospect,* foresees a
possibility of atomic blackmail by the hungry nations in
possession of nuclear secrets. He predicts these countries will
not hesitate to risk a holocaust if they don't receive a larger
share of the world's vital resources.

Such a showdown is not a misty, distant possibility, but
a fast-growing reality, of which the protest marchers near
New Delhi were an early warning. It is not difficult to understand their feelings. Their grievance is not that they
think they are entitled to outside help as a matter of natural
right, but that they are now being told, in effect, that they
are not worth helping. They are protesting lifeboat analo-
gies and the notion that some people have the right to decide whether others should live or die.

The trouble with Professor Hardin's thesis is that it is
unsound in its own terms. It defies the fact that the best way
to bring down the birthrate is not to let people starve, but to
give them a better life. . . . [This] calls for education, nutrition, decent housing, productive work. Instead of eliminating
or cutting back on aid, we ought to be stepping up shipments
of fertilizers, chemicals, plows, tractors, harvesting machines,
tools, engines, dynamos, and thousands of other items involved in upgrading living standards.

India itself is demonstrating what can be done with a
concentrated program of technological innovation. It has
cut its food deficit by a third in little more than one year.
Several model agricultural communities that have had the
benefit of adequate fertilizer and modern equipment have
increased the food yield per acre by more than 200 percent.
In light of these facts, nothing is more irresponsible or in-

competent than to say help by the outside world should
be withheld.

The principal danger of the Hardin approach will be
felt, not by India, but by the West itself. For Hardinism can
become a wild infection in the moral consciousness. If it is
possible to rationalize letting large numbers of Asians starve,
it will be no time at all before we apply the same reason-
ing to people at home. Once we discover how easy it is to
stare without flinching at famine in Calcutta or Dacca, it
should be no trick to be unblinking at the disease-ridden
tenements of Harlem or Detroit or the squalor of the shacks
in Appalachia.

Desensitization, not hunger, is the greatest curse on
earth. It begins by calibrating people's credentials to live
and ends by cheapening all life. People were appalled by
Lieutenant William Calley's moral callousness in spraying
machinegun bullets at Vietnamese. But the difference between Calley's contempt for human life and a policy of im-
passiveness toward starvation is a difference in degree and
not in values.

Famine in India and Bangladesh is a test not just of our
capacity to respond as human beings but of our ability to
understand the cycles of civilization. We can't ignore out-
stretched hands without destroying that which is most significant in the American character—a sense of vital identifi-
cation with human beings wherever they are. Regarding
life as the highest value is more important to the future of
America than anything we make or sell. We need not be
bashful in facing up to that fact and in trying to put it to
work.

A PROBLEM OF DISTRIBUTION [6]

Historically, people have tried to deny their own culpa-
bility for mass human suffering by assigning responsibility

[6] From "The World Food Problem," by Frances Moore Lappe, author of
Diet for a Small Planet. Commonweal. 99:457-9. F. 8, '74. Reprinted by permission.

to external forces beyond their control. For example, the Black Death was in large measure the result of a particular organization of society: a society that brought people together in commercial cities where it could not extend sanitation to the masses, and deforested the countryside, sending plague-laden rodents into these cities. Nevertheless, the Black Death was pronounced "Divine retribution" by the Church. Today the causes of world hunger are similarly misattributed. Current widespread climatic disasters have made it especially easy to accept natural forces as the sufficient reason for starvation.

If we accept the conclusion of many contemporary analysts that the world faces a "Malthusian food-population squeeze," then persons are indeed blameless. According to this analysis, world food problems are a function of the finite limits of Earth's resources, the vagaries of climate and an inexorable rate of population growth—all "natural" agencies, not human ones. Our response to this diagnosis is inevitably one of resignation to the apparent truth that there is simply "not enough to go around." Only if this apersonal model is true, are we freed from having to confront the human role in generating and sustaining a "world food problem." My contention is that world hunger is now, above all, a political and economic problem to which we directly contribute.

What Malthus neglected to appreciate in the late eighteenth century was that economic imbalance, not numbers of people, would come to place the greatest burden on the earth's productive capacity. He failed to foresee the enormous economic gap between the rich minority and the poor majority—a condition in which any agricultural abundance that the world could produce could just as readily be consumed by the rich minority. But then, how could Malthus have foreseen that the world would become so economically imbalanced that it would eventually be to the advantage of the rich to concentrate the world's agricultural resources on feeding animals, not people?

Today we currently feed at least 85 percent of all of our corn, barley, oats and grain sorghum, and over 90 percent of our nonexported soybean crop to livestock. We feed about 42 percent as much wheat to animals in this country as we eat ourselves, plus large quantities of wheat germ and bran. Altogether, close to one half of our agricultural acreage is now devoted to crops fed to livestock. But in addition to this plant food, American livestock are fed hundreds of thousands of tons of fishmeal and over one million tons of milk products each year.

Global figures make it even clearer that we now minimize the earth's capacity to sustain us. Consider for a moment that: (1) the rich minority of the world feeds as much grain to animals as the whole rest of humanity eats directly; (2) there is as much protein in oilseeds, that for the most part go to livestock, as there is in all the meat protein humanity consumes; and (3) nearly half of all the fish caught in the world, containing protein as good as meat, is fed to livestock. . . .

A Question of Priorities

What appears then as a problem of scarcity is actually a reflection of the uneven worldwide distribution of economic power. Extreme global inequities in the ability of nations to make demands on world food resources have made possible this pattern of highly inefficient resource use by the rich minority. But of course scarcity is also a function of the level of agricultural development, specifically (as we are now witnessing it) the vulnerability of an agricultural system to climatic disaster. But such agricultural "vulnerability" itself is a reflection of the priorities of the political and economic system.

In . . . [1973], for example, both India and China faced similar drought conditions. In India fifty million people have faced famine; in China no one has feared starvation. The reasons for this discrepancy are not hard to discern: in Maharashtra, one of the hardest hit of the Indian states, the proportion of irrigated crops has increased by only 1.5 percent in the last twenty-five years. Fifty-seven irrigation schemes that might have avoided this catastrophe were stalled for up to eight years for political and economic reasons. To date only 3 percent of India's known water reserves have been tapped. Moreover, since new "miracle" strains of grain (now used on 33 percent of India's wheat acreage and 15 percent of her rice acreage) require a greater amount of water than traditional varieties, crop yields are now more dependent on the willingness and ability of the economic and political system to provide the necessary irrigation.

China, on the other hand, has given top priority to water control for the last twenty years, with intense construction beginning in 1963. In eight years 1,700 miles of the Hai River bed were reopened or broadened. Thirty-five reservoirs which can store 106 billion cubic meters of water were built in the mountains. In addition, hundreds of thousands of wells have been bored to reach the underground water of the plains.

In this comparison the difference between adequacy and famine is not climatic events but the commitment of the political system to basic agricultural development for the majority. And here the key phrase must be "for the majority." For increased agricultural output itself does not mean the eradication of hunger. Two years ago the green revolution economists feared a "rice glut." Several Asian countries had "surplus" grain for export; but hunger was still widespread. The coexistence of "surplus" and hunger proves again the all too obvious truth that hunger is less the fault of nature than the result of an inequitable political and economic system, a system which makes it impossible for the hungry majority to buy the so-called "surplus."

But if hunger is not the result of external natural forces, then isn't it still a product of humanity's "natural," and apparently uncontrollable rate of increase that has pushed its numbers beyond the capacity of the earth? Certainly, with the world's population expected to double in the next generation, it could not long be true that there is enough to go around—even if the world's food production were distributed equitably and used efficiently. At our present land/person ratio of one acre of arable land per individual, we are reaching the limit of the earth's capacity. But this fact makes it even more imperative that we stop wasting precious time in a confused diagnosis of the problem of hunger. Hunger is not a result of current population pressures. Both rapid population growth and hunger are the reflection of the failure of a political and economic system. Neither can be solved without overall improvement in: (1) health care to reduce infant mortality and the resulting need for many births; (2) education to make fertility control understandable and widen life-goals beyond the family; (3) communication to make society-wide purposes realistic; (4) employment opportunity for both men and women to increase personal security; and (5) basic agricultural development and concomitant land income redistribution to give the majority a real stake in economic development. Thus, to label population growth as a cause of world hunger and to single it out for direct attack is a tragic illusion. The only way both can be solved is through political and economic change—the alleviation of world poverty.

V. THE ROLE OF THE UNITED STATES

EDITOR'S INTRODUCTION

America's "amber waves of grain" and "fruited plains" are indeed central to the resolution of the world food crisis. Surplus food production—actual or potential—is one of our principal blessings and strengths. With Canada, Australia, and only a few other nations, the United States enjoys a wealth of food comparable to the oil reserves of the Arab nations as a source of power over and assistance to the rest of the world. With such a capacity, what can and should the United States do?

President Ford defines America's "special responsibility" in the first article in this section. The next article describes the nation's food assistance programs and policies, known generally as the Food for Peace program.

Private help to those in need has always characterized America's reaction to world difficulties and disasters. The final two selections review the work of two of a myriad of organizations actively seeking to relieve world hunger: CARE, founded after World War II, decribed here by its executive director, Frank Goffio; and a more recently formed group, the American Freedom from Hunger Foundation.

AMERICA'S SPECIAL RESPONSIBILITY [1]

Today, the economy of the world is under unprecedented stress. We need new approaches to international cooperation to respond effectively to the problems that we face. Developing and developed countries, market and nonmarket countries—we are all a part of one interdependent economic system.

[1] From "A 'Special Responsibility,'" excerpts from address to the United Nations September 18, 1974, by President Gerald R. Ford. *War on Hunger*. 8:1-2. O. '74.

The food and oil crises demonstrate the extent of our interdependence. Many developing nations need the food surplus of a few developed nations and many industrialized nations need the oil production of a few developing nations.

Energy is required to produce food and food to produce energy, and both to provide a decent life for everyone. The problems of food and energy can be resolved on the basis of cooperation. Or can, I should say, be made unmanageable on the basis of confrontation. Runaway inflation propelled by food and oil price increases is an early-warning signal to all of us.

Let us not delude ourselves. Failure to cooperate on oil and food and inflation could spell disaster. . . . The United Nations must not and need not allow this to occur. A global strategy for food and energy is urgently required.

The United States believes four principles should guide a global approach.

First, all nations must substantially increase production. Just to maintain the present standards of living the world must almost double its output of food and energy to match the expected increase in the world's population by the end of this century. To meet aspirations for a better life, production will have to expand at a significantly faster rate than population growth.

Second, all nations must seek to achieve a level of prices which not only provides an incentive to producers but which consumers can afford. It should now be clear that the developed nations are not the only countries which demand and receive an adequate return for their goods. But it should also be clear that by confronting consumers with production restrictions, artificial pricing, and the prospect of ultimate bankruptcy, producers will eventually become the victims of their own actions.

Third, all nations must avoid the abuse of man's fundamental needs for the sake of narrow national or block advantage. The attempt by any nation to use one commodity for political purposes will inevitably tempt other countries to use their commodities for their own purposes.

Fourth, the nations of the world must assure that the poorest among us are not overwhelmed by rising prices of the imports necessary for their survival. The traditional aid donor and the increasingly wealthy oil producers must join in this effort.

The United States recognizes the special responsibility we bear as the world's largest producer of food. That is why Secretary of State Kissinger proposed from this very podium . . . a world food conference to define a global food policy. And that is one reason why we have removed domestic restrictions on food production in the United States. It has not been our policy to use food as a political weapon, despite the oil embargo and recent oil prices and production decisions.

It would be tempting for the United States, beset by inflation and soaring energy prices, to turn a deaf ear to external appeals for food assistance, or to respond with internal appeals for export controls. But, however difficult our own economic situation, we recognize that the plight of others is worse.

Americans have always responded to human emergencies in the past, and we respond here again today.

In response to [UN] Secretary General Waldheim's appeal and to help meet the long-term challenge in food, I reiterate:

☐ To help developing nations realize their aspirations to grow more of their own food, the United States will substantially increase its assistance to agricultural production programs in other countries.

☐ Next, to insure that the survival of millions of our fellow men does not depend upon the vagaries of weather, the United States is prepared to join in a worldwide effort to negotiate, establish, and maintain an international system of food reserves. This system will work best if each nation is made responsible for managing the reserves that it will have available.

□ Finally, to make certain that the more immediate needs for food are met . . . , the United States will not only maintain the amount it spends for food shipments to nations in need, but it will increase this amount . . . [in 1974].

Thus, the United States is striving to help define and help contribute to a cooperative global policy to meet man's immediate and long-term needs for food. . . .

Now is the time for oil producers to define their conception of a global policy on energy to meet the growing need and to do this without imposing unacceptable burdens on the international monetary and trade system.

A world of economic confrontation cannot be a world of political cooperation. If we fail to satisfy man's fundamental needs for energy and food, we face a threat not just to our aspirations for a better life for all our peoples but to our hopes for a more stable and a more peaceful world. By working together to overcome our common problems, mankind can turn from fear toward hope.

From the time of the founding of the United Nations, America volunteered to help nations in need, frequently as the main benefactor. We were able to do it. We were glad to do it. But as new economic forces alter and reshape today's complex world, no nation can be expected to feed all the world's hungry people. Fortunately, however, many nations are increasingly able to help. And I call on them to join with us as truly united nations in the struggle to provide more food at lower prices for the hungry and, in general, a better life for the needy of this world.

America will continue to do more than its share. But there are realistic limits to our capacities. There is no limit, however, to our determination to act in concert with other nations to fulfill the vision of the United Nations Charter—"to save succeeding generations from the scourge of war"

and "to promote social progress and better standards of life
in a larger freedom."

FOOD AID ROLE TODAY [2]

American food has served a wide variety of diplomatic
purposes: luring the Soviet Union toward detente, rewarding Pakistan for its intermediary role in the Nixon-Kissinger
opening to China, and bolstering South Vietnam's soldiers.

It also has been employed to support US foreign economic policy. In 1971, then Treasury Secretary David Kennedy promised South Korea increased food-buying credits in
return for Seoul's reduction of textile exports to the United
States. As partial payment of that pledge, the United States
recently issued South Korea a $22.8 million food aid credit
to buy rice here.

Such political uses of food aid sparked debate . . . [in
1974] in Congress, which acted to restrict politically moti-
vated food aid for the first time in the twenty-one-years history of the program.

Defenders of [Secretary of State Henry A.] Kissinger's
priorities say there is a legitimate political use for food aid,
especially since other nations use oil and raw materials to
accomplish their own economic or diplomatic ends.

Assistant Secretary of State Thomas O. Enders says the
distinction between humanitarian and political aid is, in
any case, artificial since some of both elements are always
involved in American largesse.

If American food aid can deter aggression in the Middle
East, it may be the most humanitarian assistance this country gives, State Department officials maintain.

The debate on "political" versus "humanitarian" aid is
only one of the controversies surrounding Public Law 480,
the 1954 statute under which America has distributed more

[2] From "Food Aid Role Weighed," by Dan Morgan, staff writer. *Washington
Post.* p 1+. Mr. 14, '75. © The Washington Post. Reprinted by permission.

than 200 million tons of commodities valued at $24.5 billion around the world.

That program has relieved hunger in such places as India, the Sahel region of Africa, Bangladesh and Cambodia. . . .

PL 480 also serves American self-interest: it disposes of crop surpluses, develops new markets, provides indirect subsidies to farming branches, gives business to the US shipping industry and buttresses American diplomacy.

Critics of the program's operations say there is nothing wrong with that, but they add that clearer goals and more coherent policies are needed as this country's resources become more limited.

Many Americans are confused about the nature of the program, says James T. Grant, president of the private Overseas Development Council here.

Americans supported the postwar aid to Western Europe because political, humanitarian and security motives were inseparable, he adds. Now the aims of food aid seem much less clear and the food deficits abroad seem almost endless, not temporary as they did in Europe in the late 1940s.

An Agriculture Department official said, "We haven't got a national consensus on how to handle the question of food aid."

Senator Dick Clark (Democrat, Iowa), a member of the Senate Agriculture Committee, says the ultimate solution is to develop more productive agricultural economies abroad in order to close the widening food deficit between rich and poor countries.

In the meantime, he said, "It's time we had a total look at the program and wrote a new bill. We have got to get the domestic politics out of it. We've got to get more consistency into the program, even if it means a somewhat lower level of food shipments."

Numerous officials contacted during a two-month investigation of the operations of PL 480 said that the program has become an increasingly unwieldy weapon in fighting hunger and in encouraging other nations to increase their own agricultural productivity.

A number of officials claimed the "self-help" requirements that the United States writes into many of its food aid agreements with foreign government are seldom enforced. Such agreements usually require the governments to use revenues from the local sale of the American farm commodities for development.

Several officials in foreign assistance said this was a "cosmetic." Budget officials note that revenues raised by governments anywhere go into a single pot. Thus, they question the effectiveness of the June 30, 1974, congressional ban on using the food aid funds for defense purposes.

Some American officials say that the United States could help farmers abroad if it required governments receiving food-buying loans to establish rural credit systems or give price incentives to growers.

The Administration has said repeatedly that it wants to shift its foreign aid priorities to help countries abroad produce more food. . . .

"The one thing we all agree on is that what we have done in the past—dumping huge amounts of food when we have too much and holding back when we have too little— was abominable," said a government economist who deals with the food aid program.

Clark and others say that a long-term commitment of some kind is essential. . . .

Many Administration officials say the future of the food aid program cannot be divorced from complicated decisions about world trade, Kissinger's proposed international grain reserve and price supports for American farmers.

Harald B. Malmgren, who resigned . . . [early in 1975] as deputy special trade representative at the White House, and others agree that American farmers cannot assume all the risks of producing surpluses against disasters.

Major grain producers and consumers have started negotiating on a 60-million-ton international grain reserve, in which participating countries would share responsibility for holding reserve stocks and would release them during scarcity.

The reserve would be the centerpiece of the United Nations' plan for a system of world food security, in which international food aid would be a component.

However, domestic and international politics could well decide the success or failure of the reserve plan.

Many farmers in the United States fear it could depress prices. Agriculture Secretary Earl L. Butz maintains the reserve is no answer to the perennial problem of American overproduction. However, Malmgren and some others say that it could be sold to American farmers if there was something in it for them, such as better access to European grain markets during periods of worldwide stockbuilding.

But it might be hard to persuade the Europeans to trade an easing of their economic barriers for the reserve idea, particularly as a big American grain surplus this year seems possible.

Extreme care will have to be taken to make sure that neither the reserve scheme nor future food aid serve as a substitute for expanded investment in agricultural production abroad, officials say.

Others say food aid will be needed for years to come. Lowell Hardin, agriculture specialist at the Ford Foundation, said it can act as insurance that sudden agricultural disasters will not be a "critical issue for developing nations in getting on with other elements of national planning."

Carefully applied, he added, food aid can stabilize economies abroad, fight inflation and help balance-of-payments problems of developing societies.

A former aid worker in Brazil summed up the dilemma facing US policymakers this way:

"The question is whether the 1954 mentality of dumping surpluses abroad can be tolerated in the finite world we live in now. Can the self-serving rationale for the program be admitted in the conditions we have today?"

PRIVATE HELP: CARE, INC.[3]

There are more hungry people today than ever before. The world food crisis is no longer a "menacing specter." It is here. Millions are suffering and dying from hunger or living on the knife edge of starvation, while the precarious world economy deepens the crisis. In poor nations, inflation and the energy shortage are even more critical than here at home.

The impact of the crisis brought an unprecedented challenge to CARE [Cooperative for American Relief Everywhere] during the fiscal year ending June 30, 1974. But the continuing concern of the American and Canadian people who dug deep into their pockets at the same time that they pinched pennies to combat soaring food costs at home, combined with frugal management by CARE, enabled us to help meet that challenge.

Because of contributions totaling $18,633,402, up $4,-467,722 over the same twelve-month period in the previous fiscal year, almost 29 million impoverished people in 36 countries were assisted through such CARE projects as child feeding, medical aid, nutrition education, increased food production and other self-help programs. A total of $109,-064,414 worth of supplies and services was provided, including donations from host governments, federal grants of agricultural commodities and special project funds from both the United States and Canadian governments. This means every dollar donated to CARE was stretched almost six times. . . .

Donations to CARE are a testimonial to the humanitarianism of the American and Canadian people. Central to the concept of helping people help themselves is the requirement that participating countries and individual beneficiaries invest whatever funds, materials and services they

[3] From *Twenty-eighth Annual Report, CARE, Inc., 1974,* report to board of directors, by Frank L. Goffio, executive director. CARE, Inc. 660 First Ave. New York 10016. '74. p 3. Reprinted by permission.

can in CARE programs. Over 130 such people-to-people partnership pacts were in force in nations around the world . . . [in 1973].

Following CARE's tradition established when the first food packages went to war-torn Europe in 1946, priority consideration was given to answering disaster calls and to feeding programs. To help combat the grave global food shortage, CARE accelerated a wide variety of agricultural, food processing and nutrition programs in Africa, Asia, the Middle East and Latin America.

CARE helped feed over 20 million people every day in schools, nutrition centers and other institutions. In India alone, for example, where we have our largest operation in any single country, more than 11 million children received daily supplementary feedings. In the drought-scorched African Sahel, survival biscuits and medicines were rushed to ill and famished people and well-digging programs were greatly expanded to bring water to thousands of parched villagers. And in Asia, where millions were left homeless by floods in Pakistan, CARE sent food, vitamins, blankets and other supplies free via Pakistan International Airlines.

Operations were resumed in the Arab Republic of Egypt where plans were made to build rural schools and low-cost houses as well as to set up nutrition education and school feeding programs affecting more than one million children. During his trip to the Middle East to conclude negotiations with Egyptian officials, . . . [a CARE official] also visited Israel where he reviewed CARE's current programs. Aid to these two traditional adversaries underscores our policy of extending assistance based solely on need regardless of religious belief or political consideration.

As part of its expanding healing and teaching operations, CARE-MEDICO established new programs in Belize (formerly British Honduras). In cooperation with the host government, accredited training for nurse anesthetists and X-ray technicians was conducted.

In other areas CARE began focusing on new day-care programs. By allowing adults to work while their children are cared for, and by offering basic instruction in nutrition and health care to both mothers and children, the programs are a giant step toward improving the general health and well-being of entire families.

PRIVATE HELP: AMERICAN FREEDOM FROM HUNGER FOUNDATION [4]

The American Freedom from Hunger Foundation [AFFHF] was founded in 1961 at the suggestion of President John F. Kennedy to provide a nongovernmental focal point for cooperation with the worldwide Freedom from Hunger Campaign sponsored by the Food and Agriculture Organization [FAO] of the United Nations. It has effectively mobilized private sector support for food and agricultural development programs and policies, public and private. It has worked with and provided support for governmental and nongovernmental agencies at home and abroad.

In 1963, the Foundation assisted the US Government as cohost to the FAO-sponsored nongovernmental World Food Congress held in Washington, D.C. Again in 1970 the Foundation was the focal point for mobilizing US participation in the second nongovernmental World Food Congress sponsored by the FAO in The Hague. Funds raised by the Foundation made it possible for the US delegation to include young people and others who could not otherwise participate.

The AFFHF has acted as the citizen support arm for the Food and Agriculture Organization of the United Nations, and has always maintained ex-officio liaison with the Agency for International Development and the United States Department of Agriculture. It has also contributed signifi-

---

[4] From pamphlet *American Freedom from Hunger Foundation.* The Foundation. 1100 17th St. N.W. Washington, D.C. 20036. '74. Unpaged. Reprinted by permission.

cantly on the domestic side to projects and community organizations sponsored by the Office of Economic Opportunity, Vista and the Peace Corps.

The American Freedom from Hunger Foundation seeks to arouse public awareness of the causes of hunger and malnutrition, both in the United States and abroad, and to encourage the American people to become personally involved in solving these problems. Its thrust is primarily educational . . . but it stresses education through personal and institutional commitment. Some of its specific goals are:

- ☐ To involve people in community action directed at the problem of world hunger and self-development
- ☐ To assist those government and nongovernment agencies which attempt to alleviate hunger and poverty, both domestically and internationally
- ☐ To develop grassroots support for economic aid to less developed countries, through fundraising and educational programs
- ☐ To stimulate contributions for collaborative efforts to relieve human disasters, both at home and abroad
- ☐ To encourage American leadership and response to the realities of world hunger and the international food situation

AFFHF's domestic projects are carried out in local communities across the country by various reputable nonprofit agencies. Some recent projects supported by AFFHF include:

> Research and education on Indian nutrition in North Dakota
> Inner city nutrition training center in San Diego
> Inner city day care center in Hollywood, Florida
> Day care centers in Eugene and Klamath Falls, Oregon
> Migrant workers training programs in Iowa and Minnesota
> Indian crafts program in Great Falls, Montana

Low cost housing project in suburban Chicago
Developmental reading project in Minneapolis
Economic development in Mississippi
Food cooperatives in Chicago and Buffalo
Emergency feeding program in Sacramento
High protein food supplement project in Texas

Support for Foreign Projects

Believing that poverty and hunger know no national boundaries, AFFHF supports foreign projects, too, which are carried out by qualified international organizations such as FAO, and voluntary agencies such as the Church World Service, Catholic Relief Service, CARE, and the American Friends Service Committee. Examples of programs conducted in countries outside the United States include:

Potable water and credit unions in Mexico
Agricultural training for rural youth in Tanzania
Home garden demonstrations in Malagasy
Poultry and swine vaccine equipment in Guatemala
Irrigation pumps for cooperatives in Ecuador
Rehabilitation centers in Nigeria
Community canneries in Chile
Farm youth training and veterinary educational materials in India
Farm mechanization study fellowships in Colombia
School construction in Brazil, Ghana and Peru

In its role of uniting private and public efforts to combat hunger and promote self-development, AFFHF has provided the leadership for establishing a World Hunger Action Coalition which is made up of church and development groups, private voluntary agencies operating overseas, farm and cooperative groups, food-oriented business groups and other concerned citizens. It has served as the liaison contact between US government and private groups involved in preparing for the ministerial-level World Food Conference sponsored by the United Nations. . . .

The foundation continues to sponsor food policy discussion and seminars throughout the United States, as well as specific educational programs, such as mobilizing resources for emergency assistance and long-range rehabilitation for the drought-stricken Sahel Zone in West Africa. In this case, AFFHF serves as a tax-deductible channel for public contributions to the FAO emergency trust fund and for other US agencies operating programs in the Sahel. The same facilities and support are available for emergency fundraising in other natural disasters; it is the Foundation's policy to work *with* other agencies operating relief and rehabilitation programs, rather than to compete against them. . . .

Young World Development

The Foundation points with pride to its record in motivating thousands of young Americans to "turn on" to concern for others and to maintain an awareness of the need for internationalism. As the youth component of AFFHF, Young World Development provides young people with an opportunity to learn more about world problems and to seek meaningful ways in which to become involved in related community activities.

Over the past six years, Young World Development groups have raised more than $12 million for more than one hundred international agencies and thousands of domestic poverty programs. The bulk of the money was raised through "Walks for Development"—young men and women walking at a specific rate per mile, paid by sponsors. This has proved a dramatic way to focus national attention on the world's hungry, as well as to draw personal commitments to the cause. Funds raised are turned over to AFFHF for distribution to domestic and international self-help development projects related to the causes of hunger.

VI. THE ROLE OF THE UNITED NATIONS

EDITOR'S INTRODUCTION

Central to the role of the United Nations in dealing with the world food crisis was the World Food Conference held in Rome in November 1974, in which representatives of 130 nations participated. Beyond its exchange of views and numerous resulting resolutions, the Conference served to focus the world's attention more sharply on the food supply question. The Conference in addition set in motion later action by the United Nations General Assembly to create a World Food Council to deal specifically with the crisis. Under the leadership of Dr. John A. Hannah, the Council is currently in its organization stage.

The position of the United States was eloquently expressed at the conference by Secretary of State Henry A. Kissinger, parts of whose address are reprinted in this section. The next article contains the principal declaration issued at the close of the conference, stating its goal as nothing less than the eradication of hunger.

United Nations action in this field did not start with the 1974 conference. The UN has been active throughout its existence in supporting worldwide agricultural programs and fighting hunger. The final selections in this section are concerned with this work, undertaken through the Food and Agriculture Organization, one of the UN's permanent bodies and through the United Nations International Children's Emergency Fund (UNICEF).

NO CHILD WILL GO TO BED HUNGRY [1]

We meet to address man's most fundamental need. The threat of famine, the fact of hunger have haunted men and nations throughout history. Our presence here is recognition that this eternal problem has now taken on unprecedented scale and urgency and that it can only be dealt with by concerted worldwide action. . . .

President Ford has instructed me to declare on behalf of the United States: We regard our good fortune and strength in the field of food as a global trust. We recognize the responsibilities we bear by virtue of our extraordinary productivity, our advanced technology, and our tradition of assistance. That is why we proposed this [world food] conference. That is why a secretary of state is giving this address. The United States will make a major effort to match its capacity to the magnitude of the challenge. We are convinced that the collective response will have an important influence on the nature of the world that our children inherit.

As we move toward the next century the nations assembled here must begin to fashion a global conception. For we are irreversibly linked to each other—by interdependent economies and human aspirations, by instant communications and nuclear peril. The contemporary agenda of energy, food and inflation exceeds the capacity of any single government, or even of a few governments together, to resolve. . . .

The Food Challenge

We must begin here with the challenge of food. No social system, ideology or principle of justice can tolerate a world in which the spiritual and physical potential of hundreds of millions is stunted from elemental hunger or in-

[1] From text of speech by Henry Kissinger, secretary of state, at opening session of World Food Conference in Rome on November 5, 1974. Text in *War on Hunger.* 8:1-4+. D. '74.

adequate nutrition. National pride or regional suspicions lose any moral and practical justification if they prevent us from overcoming this scourge.

A generation ago many farmers were self-sufficient—today fuel, fertilizer, capital and technology are essential for their economic survival. A generation ago many nations were self-sufficient; today a good many exporters provide the margin between life and death for many millions.

Thus food has become a central element of the international economy. A world of energy shortages, rampant inflation and a weakening trade and monetary system will be a world of food shortages as well. And food shortages in turn sabotage growth and accelerate inflation. . . .

We are convinced that the world faces a challenge new in its severity, its pervasiveness, and its global dimension. Our minimum objective of the next quarter-century must be to more than double world food production and to improve its quality. To meet this objective the United States proposes to this Conference a comprehensive program of urgent, cooperative worldwide action of five fronts:

☐ Increasing the production of food exporters
☐ Accelerating the production in developing countries
☐ Improving means of food distribution and financing
☐ Enhancing food quality
☐ Ensuring security against food emergencies

Increased Production by Food Exporters

A handful of countries, through good fortune and technology, can produce more than they need and thus are able to export. Reliance on this production is certain to grow through the next decade and perhaps beyond. Unless we are to doom the world to chronic famine, the major exporting nations must rapidly expand their potential and seek to ensure the dependable long-term growth of their supplies.

They must begin by adjusting their agricultural policies to a new economic reality. For years these policies were based on the premise that production to full capacity created undesirable surpluses and depressed markets, depriving farmers of incentives to invest and produce. It is now abundantly clear that this is not the problem we face; there is no surplus so long as there is an unmet need. In that sense, no real surplus has ever existed. The problem has always been a collective failure to transfer apparent surpluses to areas of shortages. In current and foreseeable conditions this can surely be accomplished without dampening incentives for production in either area.

The United States has taken sweeping steps to expand its output to the maximum. It already has 167 million acres under grain production alone [in 1974] an increase of 23 million acres from . . . [1972]. In an address to the Congress . . . [in November 1974], President Ford asked for a greater effort still; he called upon every American farmer to produce to full capacity. He directed the elimination of all restrictive practices which raise food prices; he assured farmers that he will use present authority and seek additional authority to allocate the fuel and fertilizer they require; and he urged the removal of remaining acreage limitations.

These efforts should be matched by all exporting countries. Maximum production will require a substantial increase in investment. The best land, the most accessible water, and the most obvious improvements are already in use. . . .

A comparable effort by other nations is essential. The United States believes that cooperative action among exporting countries is required to stimulate rational planning and the necessary increases in output. We are prepared to join with other major exporters in a common commitment to raise production, to make the necessary investment, and to begin rebuilding reserves for food security. Immediately following the conclusion of this Conference, the United States proposes to convene a group of major exporters—an export planning group—to shape a concrete and coordinated program to achieve these goals.

Accelerated Production of Developing Countries

The food exporting nations alone will simply not be able to meet the world's basic needs. Ironically but fortunately, it is the nations with the most rapidly growing food deficits which also possess the greatest capacity for increased production. They have the largest amounts of unused land and water. While they have 35 percent more land in grain production than the developed nations, they produce 20 percent less on this land. In short, the largest growth in world food production can—and must—take place in the chronic deficit countries.

Yet the gap between supply and demand in these countries is growing, not narrowing. At the current growth rate, the grain supply deficit is estimated to more than triple and reach some 85 million tons by 1985. To cut this gap in half would require accelerating their growth rate from the historically high average of 2.5 percent per annum to 3.5 percent—an increase in the rate of growth of 40 percent.

Two key areas need major emphasis to achieve even this minimum goal: new research and new investment.

International and national research programs must be concentrated on the special needs of the chronic food deficit nations and they must be intensified. New technologies must be developed to increase yields and reduce costs, making use of the special features of their labor-intensive, capital-short economies.

On the international plane, we must strengthen and expand the research network linking the less developed countries with research institutions in the industrialized countries and with the existing eight international agricultural research centers. We propose that resources for these centers be more than doubled by 1980. For its part the United States will in the same period triple its own contribution for the international centers, for agricultural research efforts in the less developed countries, and for research by American universities on the agricultural problems of developing nations. . . .

While we can hope for technological breakthroughs, we cannot count on them. There is no substitute for additional investment in chronic food-deficit countries. New irrigation systems, storage and distribution systems, production facilities for fertilizer, pesticide and seed, and agricultural credit institutions are all urgently needed. Much of this can be stimulated and financed locally. But substantial outside resources will be needed for some time to come.

The United States believes that investment should be concentrated in strategic areas, applying existing, and in some cases very simple, technologies to critical variables in the process of food production. Among these are fertilizer, better storage facilities and pesticides.

Modern fertilizer is probably the most critical single input for increasing crop yields; it is also the most dependent on new investment. In our view fertilizer production is an ideal area for collaboration between wealthier and poorer nations, especially combining the technology of developed countries, the capital and raw materials of the oil producers and the growing needs of the least developed countries. Existing production capacity is inadequate worldwide; new fertilizer industries should be created especially in the developing countries to meet local and regional needs for the long term. This could be done most efficiently on the basis of regional cooperation.

The United States will strongly support such regional efforts. In our investment and assistance programs we will give priority to the building of fertilizer industries and will share our advanced technology.

Another major priority must be to reduce losses from inadequate storage, transport, and pest control. Tragically, as much as 15 percent of a country's food production is often lost after harvesting because of pests that attack grains in substandard storage facilities. Better methods of safe

storage must be taught and spread as widely as possible.
Existing pesticides must be made more generally available.
Many of these techniques are simple and inexpensive; investment in these areas could have a rapid and substantial
impact on the world's food supply.

To plan a coherent investment strategy, the United
States proposes the immediate formation of a coordinating
group for food production and investment. We recommend
that the World Bank join with the Food and Agriculture
Organization and the UN Development Program to convene
such a group this year. . . .

Improving Food Distribution and Financing

While we must urgently produce more food, the problem of its distribution will remain crucial. Even with maximum foreseeable agricultural growth in the developing
countries, their food import requirement is likely to amount
to some 40 million tons a year in the mid-1980s, or nearly
twice the current level.

How is the cost of these imports to be met?

The earnings of the developing countries themselves, of
course, remain the principal source. The industrialized nations can make a significant contribution simply by improving access to their markets. With the imminent passage of
the trade bill, the United States reaffirms its commitment to
institute a system of generalized tariff preferences for the
developing nations and to pay special attention to their
needs in the coming multilateral trade negotiations.

Nevertheless, an expanded flow of food aid will clearly
be necessary. During this fiscal year, the United States will
increase its food aid contribution, despite the adverse
weather conditions which have affected our crops. The
American people have a deep and enduring commitment
to help feed the starving and the hungry. We will do everything humanly possible to assure that our future contribution will be responsive to the growing needs.

The responsibility for financing food imports cannot,

however, rest with the food exporters alone. Over the next few years in particular, the financing needs of the food-deficit developing countries will simply be too large for either their own limited resources or the traditional food aid donors.

The oil exporters have a special responsibility in this regard. Many of them have income far in excess of that needed to balance their international payments or to finance their economic development. The continuing massive transfer of wealth and the resulting impetus to worldwide inflation have shattered the ability of the developing countries to purchase food, fertilizer and other goods. And the economic crisis has severely reduced the imports of the industrialized countries from the developing nations.

The United States recommends that the traditional donors and the new financial powers participating in the coordinating group for food production and investment make a major effort to provide the food and funds required. They could form a subcommittee on food financing which, as a first task, would negotiate a minimum global quantity of food for whose transfer to food-deficit developing countries over the next three years they are prepared to find the necessary finances. . . .

Ensuring Against Food Emergencies

The events of the past few years have brought home the grave vulnerability of mankind to food emergencies caused by crop failures, floods, wars and other disasters. The world has come to depend on a few exporting countries, and particularly the United States, to maintain the necessary reserves. But reserves no longer exist, despite the fact that the United States has removed virtually all of its restrictions on production and our farmers have made an all-out effort to maximize output. A worldwide reserve of as much as 60 million tons of food above present carryover levels may be needed to assure adequate food security.

It is neither prudent nor practical for one or even a

few countries to be the world's sole holder of reserves. Nations with a history of radical fluctuations in import requirements have an obligation, both to their own people and to the world community, to participate in a system which shares that responsibility more widely. And exporting countries can no longer afford to be caught by surprise. They must have advance information to plan production and exports.

We recommend FAO Director General Boerma for his initiative in the area of reserves. The United States shares his view that a cooperative multilateral system is essential for greater equity and efficiency. We therefore propose that this Conference organize a Reserves Coordinating Group to negotiate a detailed agreement on an international system of nationally held grain reserves at the earliest possible time. It should include all the major exporters as well as those whose import needs are likely to be greatest. This group's work should be carried out in close cooperation with other international efforts to improve the world trading system.

An International Reserve System should include the following elements:

- —Exchange of information on levels of reserve and working stocks, on crop prospects and on intentions regarding imports and exports
- —Agreement on the size of global reserves required to protect against famine and price fluctuations
- —Sharing of the responsibility for holding reserves
- —Guidelines on the management of national reserves, defining the conditions for adding to reserves and for releasing from them
- —Preference for cooperating countries in the distribution of reserves
- —Procedures for adjustment of targets and settlement of disputes and measures for dealing with noncompliance . . .

Conclusion

Nothing more overwhelms the human spirit, or mocks our values and our dreams, than the desperate struggle for sustenance. No tragedy is more wounding than the look of despair in the eyes of a starving child.

Once famine was considered part of the normal cycle of man's existence, a local or at worst a national tragedy. Now our consciousness is global. Our achievements, our expectations, and our moral convictions have made this issue into a universal political concern.

The profound promise of our era is that for the first time we may have the technical capacity to free mankind from the scourge of hunger. Therefore, today we must proclaim a bold objective—that within a decade no child will go to bed hungry, that no family will fear for its next day's bread, and that no human being's future and capacities will be stunted by malnutrition.

THE ERADICATION OF HUNGER [2]

The World Food Conference, convened by the General Assembly of the United Nations and entrusted with developing ways and means whereby the international community, as a whole, could take specific action to resolve the world food problem within the broader context of development and international economic cooperation, adopts the following Universal Declaration on the Eradication of Hunger and Malnutrition. . . .

The Conference consequently solemnly proclaims:
    1. Every man, woman and child has the inalienable

[2] "Declaration on the Eradication of Hunger and Malnutrition," adopted by the World Food Conference on November 16, 1974. In *Report on the World Food Conference: Hearing Before the Committee on Foreign Affairs, House of Representatives,* November 26, 1974. 93d Congress, 2d session. Supt. of Docs. Washington, D.C. 20402. '74. p 42-5.

right to be free from hunger and malnutrition in order to develop fully and maintain their physical and mental faculties. Society today already possesses sufficient resources, organizational ability, and technology and hence the competence to achieve this objective. Accordingly, the eradication of hunger is a common objective of all the countries of the international community, especially of the developed countries and others in a position to help.

2. It is a fundamental responsibility of governments to work together for higher food production and a more equitable and efficient distribution of food between countries and within countries. Governments should initiate immediately a greater concerted attack on chronic malnutrition and deficiency diseases among the vulnerable and lower income groups. In order to ensure adequate nutrition for all, governments should formulate appropriate food and nutrition policies integrated in overall socioeconomic and agricultural development plans based on adequate knowledge of available as well as potential food resources. The importance of human milk in this connection should be stressed on nutritional grounds.

3. Food problems must be tackled during the preparation and implementation of national plans and programs for economic and social development, with emphasis on their humanitarian aspects.

4. It is a responsibility of each state concerned, in accordance with its sovereign judgment and internal legislation, to remove the obstacles to food production and provide proper incentives to agricultural producers. Of prime importance for the attainment of these objectives are effective measures of socioeconomic transformation by agrarian, tax, credit and investment policy reform and the reorganization of rural structures, such as the reform of the conditions of ownership, the encouragement of producer and consumer cooperatives, the mobilization of the full potential of human resources, both male and female, in the developing

countries for an integrated rural development and the involvement of the small farmers, fishermen and the landless workers in attaining the required food production and employment targets. Moreover, it is necessary to recognize the key role of women in agricultural production and rural economy in many countries, and to ensure that appropriate education, extension programs and financial facilities are made available to women on equal terms with men.

5. Marine and inland water resources are today becoming more important than ever as a source of food and economic prosperity. Accordingly, action should be taken to promote a rational exploitation of these resources, preferably for direct human consumption, in order to contribute to meeting the food requirements of all peoples.

6. The efforts to increase food production should be complemented by every endeavor to prevent wastage of food in all its forms.

7. To give impetus to food production in developing countries and in particular in the least developed and most seriously affected among them, urgent and effective international action should be taken, by the developed countries and other countries in a position to do so, to provide them with sustained additional technical and financial assistance on favorable terms and in a volume sufficient to their needs on the basis of the bilateral and multilateral arrangements. This assistance must be free of conditions inconsistent with sovereignty of the receiving states.

8. All countries, and primarily the highly industrialized countries, should promote the advancement of food production technology and should make all efforts to promote the transfer, adaptation and dissemination of appropriate food production technology for the benefit of the developing countries and to that end they should *inter alia* make all efforts to disseminate the results of their research work to governments and scientific institutions of developing countries in order to enable them to promote a sustained agricultural development.

9. To assure the proper conservation of natural resources being utilized or utilizable for food production, all countries must collaborate in order to facilitate the preservation of the environment, including the marine environment.

10. All developed countries and others able to do so should collaborate technically and financially with the developing countries in their efforts to expand land and water resources for agricultural production and to assure a rapid increase in the availability, at fair costs, of agricultural inputs such as fertilizers and other chemicals, high-quality seeds, credit and technology. Cooperation among developing countries, in this connection, is also important.

11. All states should strive to the utmost to readjust, where appropriate, their agricultural policies to give priority to food production recognizing, in this connection, the interrelationship between the world food problem and international trade. In the determination of attitudes toward farm support programs for domestic food production, developed countries should take into account, as far as possible, the interest of the food exporting developing countries, in order to avoid detrimental effect on their exports. Moreover, all countries should cooperate to devise effective steps to deal with the problem of stabilizing world markets and promoting equitable and remunerative prices, where appropriate through international agreements, to improve access to markets through reduction or elimination of tariff and nontariff barriers on the products of interest to the developing countries, to substantially increase the export earnings of these countries, to contribute to the diversification of their exports, and apply to them, in the multilateral trade negotiations, the principles as agreed upon in the Tokyo Declaration including the concept of nonreciprocity and more favorable treatment.

12. As it is the common responsibility of the entire international community to ensure the availability at all times of adequate world supplies of basic foodstuffs by way

of appropriate reserves including emergency reserves, all countries should cooperate in the establishment of an effective system of world food security by:

☐ participating in and supporting the operation of the Global Information and Early Warning System on Food and Agriculture

☐ adhering to the objectives, policies and guidelines of the proposed International Undertaking on World Food Security as endorsed by the World Food Conference

☐ ear-marking, where possible, stocks or funds for meeting international emergency food requirements as envisaged in the proposed International Undertaking on World Food Security and developing international guidelines to provide for the coordination and the utilization of such stocks

☐ cooperating in the provision of food aid for meeting emergency and nutritional needs as well as for stimulating rural employment through development projects

All donor countries should accept and implement the concept of forward planning of food aid and make all efforts to provide commodities and/or financial assistance that will ensure adequate quantities of grains and other food commodities. Time is short. Urgent and sustained action is vital. The Conference, therefore, calls upon all peoples expressing their will as individuals, and through their governments and nongovernmental organizations, to work together to bring about the end of the age-old scourge of hunger.

The Conference affirms:

The determination of the participating states to make full use of the United Nations system in the implementation of this Declaration and the other decisions adopted by the Conference.

FOOD AND AGRICULTURE ORGANIZATION [3]

The Food and Agriculture Organization of the United Nations is an agency for international action, to fight the poverty, malnutrition and hunger which afflict about half the people in the world.

It is an independent organization in the United Nations family of specialized agencies.

It is a cooperative of 131 governments pooling their efforts to meet the needs of nearly 4,000 million people alive today and of perhaps 6,500 million by the end of the century.

It is a force of men and women working all over the world to gauge the extent and complexity of the food problem and to help solve it by providing advice and technical assistance and by helping to mobilize capital backing for development programs. . . .

FAO Is a Source of Information and Advice

Knowledge is basic to the solution of any problem. In two decades FAO has become an international center of information on every aspect of agriculture, fisheries, forestry and nutrition. Statistics on production, trade and consumption of hundreds of commodities are gathered from all over the world and published in statistical reviews and yearbooks. Food balance sheets show supplies of food available to the people of many countries and the world nutritional situation is reviewed in periodic world food surveys. There are monographs bringing together the results of scientific research published in many languages; there are reporting services on the outbreak and spread of plant and animal diseases; there are catalogs of tractors and sawmill equipment available from many countries; there are lists of plant breeders and tree seed suppliers; there are studies of the

[3] From "FAO: What It Is, What It Does, How It Works." Food and Agriculture Organization of the United Nations. Rome. '74. Unpaged. Reprinted by permission.

economic outlook for commodities ranging from fish meal and sawn timber to silk and spices.

To an increasing extent in recent years FAO has drawn attention to the policy implications of the information it provides. Not content with merely describing the present situation, it also attempts to assess future developments and to suggest policy measures to improve the future. . . .

FAO is . . . developing policy guidelines for a system of minimum world food security. In response to the serious fall in grain reserves following the very poor harvests of 1972, the director-general of FAO proposed that all countries, both developed and less developed, should cooperate in building up national food stocks against future crop failures. The [governing] conference backed these proposals and asked the secretariat to assist in the preparation of a world food security scheme for adoption by governments. . . .

FAO has also played a leading part in providing basic studies and secretariat support for the United Nations World Food Conference called in Rome in November 1974 to discuss and agree on international action to deal with the rundown in the world's food reserves and the growing shortages and rising prices of chemical fertilizers which occurred in the early 1970s. . . .

FAO Is an Action Program

Above all, FAO is an agency for action. In the end, food production increases must be achieved on the farm and the seas. Many people are hungry and ill fed in the towns and villages of the developing world. And it is there that more than 2,000 technicians—or about two out of three professional staff—are working today.

Most of FAO's field activities have grown out of the United Nations Expanded Programme of Technical Assistance, established in 1950, and the UN Special Fund, established in 1958; these two programs were later merged into the United Nations Development Programme (UNDP).

UNDP provides not only skilled technicians but also pays for equipment and provides fellowship funds to enable technicians from assisted countries to study abroad.

It is not an aid program imposed on a country from abroad. Countries are informed of the amount of UNDP funds which they can expect over a five-year period and then, in consultation with international advisers, they decide on the overall program of aid and advice from all the UN agencies that will meet their major needs. FAO specialists, and especially the FAO Senior Agricultural Advisers based in about fifty countries, have helped to draw up 102 country programs prepared in 1972 and 1973. These 102 programs call for the expenditure of UNDP funds amounting to US $1,061 million over the period 1972–76 and FAO was chosen to execute projects involving about $318 million or about 30 percent of the total UNDP allocations; other agencies in the UN family were to carry out the other programs. . . .

Typical UNDP projects executed by FAO are:

☐ In Nigeria, the Savanna Forestry Research project has assisted in the establishment of a viable research station, now almost wholly staffed by nationals; and a fisheries project has contributed to a substantial increase in the catch of sea fish and thus to an increase in the incomes of local fishermen.

☐ In central Tunisia, FAO and the World Food Programme [WFP], working together, have helped the rural community particularly by the wide-scale planting of fruit trees and the development of forage crops.

☐ In Ethiopia, FAO has assisted in the establishment of the country's first Agricultural Research Institute: it has undertaken research and helped national staff, through in-service training and a large program of fellowships, to reach a high standard of scientific competence.

☐ FAO continues to administer an institute linking a

chain of animal health institutes in thirteen countries
of the Near East; this has now reached a stage where
nationals of the region are beginning to take over
responsibility for the work of this institute, and will
be entirely responsible within the next few years. The
institutes have proved invaluable in helping to control the spread of animal diseases throughout the region as well as to individual countries.

☐ In Peru, FAO is supporting training and research
work in agrarian reform, and is helping in the development of forest industries.

☐ A series of regional projects surveying the Senegal
River basin have produced plans for the integrated
development of irrigation, river transport and power
production; it is expected that these will soon lead
to investment action, including a dam on the lower
river to provide irrigation and prevent intrusion of
seawater.

☐ In Malaysia, FAO is helping the government prepare
long-term plans for the development of forests and
forest industries. The Organization is also helping to
staff and administer a Malaysian Forestry College to
train intermediate-level foresters for the national forest service.

☐ In addition to the expertise supplied by FAO field
staff and associate experts, about sixty volunteers
work in FAO's field activities, an increasing majority
being assigned under the auspices of the United Nations Volunteer Programme with the rest serving under direct arrangements with the sponsors.

Since 1963, FAO has cosponsored with the United Nations the outstandingly successful World Food Programme
which uses food itself in support of development. Given as
a family ration in part-payment of wages to men planting
trees, digging irrigation channels, building roads, schools,
houses, etc., it reduces the wage bill, increases employment

and encourages healthy food habits, thus contributing to
economic growth. Food is given to settlers on new land until
they harvest their first crops and to industrial workers to
help build up productivity.

When distributed through hospitals, child care centers
and schools, it helps the vulnerable groups of population
and encourages attendance at school while it keeps children
in better health to gain the most from their lessons.

The resources available to WFP since its inception, including pledges for the period 1973–74, reached a total of
$1,199,096,643 by the end of December 1973. Of these, $886,-
565,647 were in food commodities and the balance in cash
and services. A further $83,360,568 worth of food grains
were made available to the program by signatories to the
Food Aid Convention. Big increases in cereal and other
food prices from 1972 onward, however, have compelled
WFP to scale down its planned program.

A total of 591 projects in 88 countries had been ap-
proved at a total cost of $1,374,983,622. In addition, 174
emergency food aid operations had been undertaken in 74
countries at a total cost to the program of $133,488,842.

In its first decade, WFP helped to produce some impressive results in eighty countries throughout the third world:

—nearly 1 million hectares of arid, overgrazed or fallow
land reclaimed and brought under crops or timber
—422,200 housing units built or renovated
—5,700 schools and 7,000 public buildings constructed
—25,840 kilometers of rural roads and 7,750 kilometers of
urban streets built or repaired
—1,120 bridges built
—1,460 kilometers of railway track laid or repaired
—650 kilometers of power lines laid
—21,000 kilometers of canals built or repaired and another 667,600 kilometers of canals cleared of salt and
regularly maintained
—200 kilometers of flood protection dikes completed

—25,000 wells dug for supply of drinking water and irrigation
—200,000 refugees helped to resettle
—3,700,000 students in primary and secondary schools, literacy classes and training centers provided with meals
—207,000 mothers and 735,000 infants given nutritious diets

About 3.4 million workers are estimated to have received food and in one year alone some 900,000 full-time jobs were created.

A small part of WFP food is used for meeting emergency food needs in the wake of disasters, e.g., floods, typhoons, earthquakes or droughts. The biggest single emergency relief operation has been in the Sahelian Zone of west Africa where persistent low rainfall over the past years has caused the worst drought in living memory.

The World Food Programme was first established for a three-year trial term. Since then it has so conclusively proved itself that the United Nations and FAO have decided to continue it for as long as multilateral food aid is found feasible and desirable.

FAO Is Also a People's Program

Most of FAO's work is carried on in cooperation with governments, but governments alone cannot solve the world food problem. And so, in 1960, FAO launched the Freedom from Hunger Campaign to provide a role for the private citizen in the war on poverty. Today the campaign is carried on by nearly one hundred national committees and with the support of more than one hundred other nongovernmental groups. In recognition of the fact that hunger is just one of the elements of the overall problem of development, the name of the program has been expanded to Freedom from Hunger Campaign/Action for Development [FFHC/AD].

The primary aim of the campaign is to enlarge public consciousness of the extent and causes of world hunger and poverty. It is an attempt to bring people everywhere to realize that the problem of world and social development is everybody's problem. It is an attempt to help every person and group to identify the role they can play in the process of development and to stimulate them to do whatever they can.

The campaign has made a particular effort to attract the support of young people who have shown themselves especially concerned with the problems of development today and who will carry full responsibility for their solution tomorrow.

The campaign also provides an opportunity to the individual to involve himself in development and to learn more about its mechanics through financing development programs. In 1973 there were 157 FFHC/AD projects in operation including 30 new projects adopted by voluntary agencies during the year. Voluntary contributions during the year totaled $2.8 million. Even larger sums have gone to FFHC projects not passing through FAO.

The priority aim of an FFHC project is that it should mobilize human effort for self-development. It is always intended that FFHC projects should be a direct answer to local needs, that they should involve the beneficiaries from the outset, and that it should be likely and possible for them to be continued by local people once outside assistance is terminated. As far as possible, priority is given to projects which call for social as well as technical and economic answers to development problems.

U.N. INTERNATIONAL CHILDREN'S EMERGENCY FUND [4]

How can an organization like UNICEF [United Nations International Children's Emergency Fund] help the many hungry children in the world? UNICEF doesn't have enough

[4] From "What Can UNICEF Do?". *UNICEF's World*. No. 1102:2. '74. Reprinted by permission of United States Committee for UNICEF.

money or resources to solve all the problems or to fight the emergency alone. But it can help in several ways and make a real difference in the lives of many children.

For the past twenty-seven years, since UNICEF was created, it has worked to provide children with more food and with better food. And it has learned a lot over the years. It has learned the things that can be done now to give immediate help and the other things that can be done to provide help in the future.

Imagine that you are the executive director of UNICEF, and you have to decide how UNICEF can best help millions of hungry children in poor countries far away. You have to figure out the ways to help people in the countryside and in small villages get the food they need. Think about these things for a few moments before you read on.

Your first thought might be to simply send food on planes or ships. That's one way to provide help now. But it's more complicated than it might seem at first.

Sending food to the millions who need it is very expensive. Not only the food itself, but the cost of transportation. And then there's the difficult matter of getting the food to the people once it arrives in a country. Most of these less developed countries have few highways, railroads, or airports. Foods that children need, such as milk or vegetables, might spoil by the time they get to the right place. Sending cans of food wouldn't solve the problem, as cans are heavy and very expensive to send. These are some of the reasons why people are discouraged from donating food to UNICEF.

However, despite all the difficulties, UNICEF must send some food to the needy areas. To prevent malnutrition and starvation, special foods for children are needed. Foods that don't spoil quickly, are easy to prepare, and contain important proteins and vitamins. One such food is CSM, named for its ingredients: Corn flour, Soy flour and Milk powder. This food is saving many children's lives in Bangladesh, Vietnam, and West Africa.

Sending food is necessary in areas where immediate relief

is needed, but it isn't a solution to the problem. Today, when food shortages are growing throughout the world, we can't count on there being enough to send. And once we stop sending it, these people are often right back where they started. We need some long-term solutions.

One solution to the food problem is a lasting supply of food. Of course, UNICEF alone can't provide the solution. But UNICEF can help by teaching people to use every small plot of land they have to produce more of their own food. In 1973 UNICEF helped train approximately 97,000 nutrition workers in needy areas. These workers teach others in their communities or villages how to grow nutritious foods locally and what kinds of food are important to eat.

Even children are taught these things. In many countries, a common sight outside a village school is a garden. UNICEF sends seeds and garden tools, and all the children in the school are required to plant and to tend the vegetables. The result of their efforts helps provide their school lunch. . . .

In some areas, the land isn't fertile, and more than tools and seeds are needed. A common problem is a lack of water. UNICEF often sends pumps, pipes, and other equipment needed for village wells. These wells can irrigate small community or school gardens and also provide a clean source of drinking water.

It's also important to help people store their food properly so that it isn't wasted. In many areas, more than 20 percent of the food produced is lost to rats, mice, and other pests; or it simply spoils. Better storage is one of the quickest ways to increase food supply.

So you can see that if you were the executive director of UNICEF you would want to help the most needy areas by sending food right away. But you would also need to help people produce more nutritious food in the future. You would see what a big job it is to help the world's children, and you would realize how important the young people are who help UNICEF around the world.

VII. THE PATHS AHEAD

EDITOR'S INTRODUCTION

Crucial questions remain. Will the world food crisis be successfully resolved? When? How? This section offers some answers.

As an introduction, Professor Robert Huke, a noted geographer, takes a look at the year 2000 to see what we can expect. There follows an exhortatory message from the director general of the Food and Agriculture Organization of the United Nations, Addeke H. Boerma.

Time outlines the many options available for solution of the crisis, and Martin McLaughlin offers proposals for a world food policy.

In the concluding selection, Orville Freeman, former United States Secretary of Agriculture, proposes a global plan involving the marshaling of resources, capital, and know-how to meet our current and future needs.

ONE VIEW OF THE WORLD IN THE YEAR 2000 [1]

Twenty-five years from now world population will number at least 6.4 billion, a number equal to today's figure plus the total world population of 1950. In the next two and one-half decades alone the increase in numbers of human beings will equal the growth of the previous 40,000 years. In arriving at this figure I have assumed that efforts directed toward population control will be doubled each decade so that annual population growth will be slowed from 2.0 percent to slightly less than 1.9 percent. Rapid

[1] From position paper prepared by Professor Robert E. Huke, chairman, geography department, Dartmouth College, for Wright-Ingraham Institute workshop sponsored by the Charles F. Kettering Foundation, held near La Paz, Mexico, on January 14-17, 1975. Dartmouth College. Department of Geography. Hanover, N.H. 03755. mimeo. '75. p 1-4. Reprinted by permission.

growth appears inevitable and, in light of the attitude expressed by many delegates at [the World Population Conference at] Bucharest and decreased funding of the population program in India, there seems little possibility of slowing the growth significantly.

Paralleling the inexorable ballooning of human numbers will be increasing efforts in plant breeding and a new emphasis on agricultural technologies, especially for those vast areas of the world where yields per unit area remain abysmal. Early successes of the green revolution made possible increasing food production during the 1960s at a rate slightly in excess of population growth over much of Asia. In the coming two and one-half decades agricultural scientists will develop in a variety of food plants increased resistance to a broad range of diseases, pests, variations in temperature and moisture supply as well as a greater tolerance to soil conditions. At the same time social scientists will learn how best to adapt these innovations to agricultural societies where the traditional attitude has been minimization of risk rather than maximization of output. The result of these twin efforts will be reflected in increased production per unit area of close to 3 percent per year. By the year 2000 land in agriculture will produce, on the average, twice the food it now produces. Unfortunately the operative words in this conclusion are *land in agriculture*.

The world in 1975 cultivates some 1.4 billion hectares or almost 11 percent of the land surface (Antarctica excluded). At the same date, man's artifacts—homes, factories, dumps, roads, parking lots and the like—occupy .4 billion hectares or about 3 percent of the surface. If, as appears likely, people in the year 2000 are as demanding of space as are each of us today then an additional .3 billion hectares will be covered twenty-five years from now. This land will not be subtracted from the Siberian tundra or from the Tibetan plateau but will be located where people prefer to live. It will be removed from the most productive of our present farmed area. The .3 billion additional hectares required for living space is roughly the equivalent of the 1975 total of all farmed land in North and South America combined. Where will we find cultivable land to replace this loss? And at what price?

During the same twenty-five-year period the world agricultural base will lose still another .3 billion hectares to erosion, salinization, water logging and laterization [development of clay substance]. Such losses will not be from the most highly productive lands but will be from widely scattered marginal farming areas. These losses will be balanced by gradual incursion into the ever-shrinking reserves of forest and grassland. Game reserves and wild areas will be sacrificed at an accelerating rate to provide the calories and proteins so essential to man's continuing multiplication.

Discounting losses in storage, processing, transporting, distributing and cooking, today's 1.4 billion hectares of farmed land produce some 3.9×10^{15} kilocalories of food for human consumption or somewhat less than 1×10^6 kilocalories per capita. The position outlined in the paragraphs above postulates a doubling of productivity per unit area of farmed land; a population increase to 6.4×10^9; and a decline in farm land to 1.1×10^9 hectares. Under these conditions the food available at the farm gate on a per capita basis in 2000 A.D. will be even less than is available in 1975 and the problems of storing, transporting and distributing will make solutions to today's problems appear as child's play.

To arrive at the year 2000 in a position even as fortuitous as postulated above assumes that natural cycles of temperature and rainfall continue in at least as benign a pattern as they have followed for the first two thirds of the twentieth century and that man does nothing to further harm the environment and, in fact, that he undoes much of the damage already inflicted on the ecosystem. It is unlikely that either of these assumptions is more than wishful thinking.

In the past decade there have been a number of firm indications that mean temperatures in the northern hemisphere are declining at an alarming rate. In part this is surely in line with nature's long term pattern but with equal assurance it can be stated that man's activity is contributing significantly to . . . [this] decrease. . . .

A decrease of roughly 1°F. has been documented since 1955 and several writers feel that within the next decade or two the cooling trend could equal 1°C. Such a change would have profound effects on world agriculture. Study of the daily minimum temperatures over a fifteen-year period for stations in Vermont indicates that the frost-free period would be shortened by 7 days with a decrease in mean annual temperature of 1°F. and by 12 or 13 days with a decrease of 1°C. Similar results were found by R. E. Lautzenheiser of the New England River Basins Commission for seven states.

A decline of 1°C. in mean temperature would affect crop patterns all over the world. The effect would be least in the tropics but even here the area able to produce such temperature sensitive plants as coconut and oil palm would shrink somewhat. A mid-latitude example is Florida citrus; in the heart of the orange area a 1°C. cooling would double the likelihood of a killing frost. The most serious impact however would be a retreat of the poleward frontier of agriculture in the high latitudes. In the Canadian Prairie Provinces a twelve-day decrease in the frost-free period with no change in agricultural technology would shrink the wheat belt by one third or from 9 to 6 million hectares with a resultant loss in yield of 5 million metric tons per year. . . .

As population increases and the world food situation becomes more serious an obvious area for conservation is in the production of animal protein. The food conversion ratio for beef is roughly 8:1 and for pork about 5:1; however the ratio for farm-raised fish is seldom higher than 2:1. The production of farm raised fish including tilapia, carp, catfish and trout is increasing remarkably in Asia and Africa and in the United States is the most rapidly expanding sector of the farm economy. Annual yields of over 2,200 kg. of fish per hectare are achieved routinely and figures exceeding this by an order of magnitude are obtained from controlled environments. By the year 2000 farm-raised fish products may provide as much as 15 or 20 percent of the United States' and of the world's animal protein.

Not only are fish more efficient converters than other animals but they are also adaptable to very small and very intensive production techniques.

As food prices continue to rise and the pressure on land resources continues to increase I expect to see the development of even more intensive production techniques on the most favorably located sites. Increasing levels of agricultural inputs combined with higher transportation costs will encourage the concentration of agricultural production, other than grain, in areas close to the centers of consumption. Human population has already gone through this spatial transformation with the rapid growth of cities; perhaps the agricultural implosion could be called the urbanization of agriculture.

I have in mind the rapid expansion of controlled environment enclosures—greenhouses if you like—at the urban fringes, in the suburbs and in the rural nonfarm areas [see "The Negev Blooms," in Section III, above]. In some locations these would be large structures to provide vegetables and fish for one hundred or more families. In the suburbs and the more rural areas the structures will be designed to provide part of the needs for a single family. The surface area in such structures will be one half water (about three feet deep) and one half soil. The water will provide the habitat for food fish and will also act as a heat sink to help reduce temperature variations and lengthen the growing season. The soil will be fertilized with sludge from the local sewage plant and watered with the waste-enriched effluent from the fish tank filter. The four day work week will leave ample time for operation of the units. Solar energy will provide the major nonhuman input and the semiclosed

system will allow for the exclusion of major atmospheric
pollutants. The microworld of the dome farm and the individual contact with living systems will help to overcome
the psychological rigors of a crowded world and will help
in a small way to provide an improved diet.

Feeding 6.4 billion humans will not be easy. Success
will depend on the achievement of significant genetic and
agronomic advances on the research farms and very hard
work by social scientists to implement these technologies
on the production farms. Shrinking of the arable base will
lead to even more intensive land use patterns and a trend
toward self-sufficiency.

NEEDED: THE WILL TO SOLVE [2]

One of the articles of the [Universal] Declaration [of
Human Rights adopted by the United Nations] . . . [pro-
claims] that "everyone has the right to a standard of living
adequate for the health and well-being of himself and of his
family." Among the necessary components of this right, the
first to be mentioned was food.

There are many people in the world, especially in the
richer countries, who will regard this as a fine statement of
the obvious. There are many others, especially in the poorer
countries, who will also regard it as a fine statement, but of
a remote ideal. For the fact is that the world has never come
anywhere close to a situation in which everyone has had
enough food for an adequate standard of living. Neither in
the more distant past, nor . . . since the Universal Declaration was adopted, nor today. Today, in fact, there are
grounds for believing that . . . the situation has actually become worse. . . .

Let me reach back . . . and echo once more the challenge
thrown out by President Kennedy to the First World Food

[2] From "Solving the World's Food Problem," by Addeke H. Boerma, director
general, Food and Agriculture Organization of the United Nations. *Futurist*.
8:65-7. Ap. '74. Reprinted by permission of *The Futurist*, published by the World
Future Society, P.O. Box 30369 (Bethesda), Washington, D.C. 20014.

Congress in Washington. "We have the means," he said, "we have the capacity to eliminate hunger from the face of the earth in our lifetime. We need only the will."

Only the will, he said. But that is just what has been lacking—the political will to make the kind of radical changes that are necessary if the less fortunate members of the human family are not to continue to go short of the most basic human need. It is still lacking.

It may be asked what kind of changes I have in mind. There are certain ones which are evidently paramount and pressing.

In the first place, the world must take more energetic and intensive measures to slow down the present headlong rate of population growth, especially in the developing countries. While it is true that the world has the technological capacity to feed many more than the present population of this planet, do not think that the ghost of Malthus has been exorcised. For technology is only one factor in the food and population equation.

Next, it is essential that the world's agriculture should be viewed in terms of the world as a whole and not, as at present, so largely through the perspective of the interests of individual countries.

Thirdly, the richer countries simply must increase their foreign aid, especially to the poorest and especially where it could lead to a really important breakthrough in agricultural production. It has been estimated, for example, that an investment of $1.5 billion for the elimination of the tsetse fly in infested areas of tropical Africa could open up 4.5 million square miles to livestock and crop production.

Unemployment Is Biggest Cause of Hunger

And finally, among my list of the most important changes, every possible step must be taken to cure the vast and spreading plague of unemployment in the developing countries which, by depriving so many millions of people of purchasing power, is the most pervasive cause of hunger.

As I say, it is technically well within our grasp to increase agricultural production on an immense scale. But so far the nations of the world have not chosen to act in concert to do so in such a way that those who are the victims of hunger and malnutrition can really benefit. This is not only tragic but dangerous. For the availability of sufficient food for all the people of this world is a vital component of world economic security. And, as such, it is increasingly a condition of world peace.

What are the facts about the present world food situation? The general background is that over a quarter of a century, from the end of the Second World War to the beginning of the present decade, the increase in food production in the world generally kept up with population growth.

World Depends on North America

But this statement already conceals a vast discrepancy. In a very few countries, almost entirely in North America, grain production leaped ahead resulting in large surplus stocks that provided the world with both a security reserve against shortages and comparative price stability for the main temperate zone foodstuffs. In consequence, the world has allowed itself to drift into a dangerous degree of dependence on the prowess exercised on the plains of North America.

In the developing countries, the increase in food production just managed to stay abreast of population growth for most of the period. This was a considerable achievement, but the situation was generally precarious, and it has also to be remembered that the vast majority of the millions of hungry I have mentioned live in those countries. . . .

Painful Scarcities and Rocketing Prices

The general situation has had extremely painful results in many parts of the world—most painful of course in some particularly vulnerable areas of the developing world, such as the Sahelian zone of west Africa and Bangladesh, where widespread famine has only been averted with the help of emergency supplies, large quantities of which came from the United States.

But almost everywhere the effects of this unprecedented situation have been felt, chiefly in the form of fiercely rising prices. There are of course general inflationary pressures, particularly in the developed countries; but these can only account in very small measure for the fact that wheat prices, for example, . . . [were in 1973] about three times what they were in the summer of 1972. And not only cereals have been affected. With the dependence of the livestock industry on grain, the prices of meat, as citizens of even this richest nation on earth are only too grimly aware, have been rocketing. Price increases in a large number of countries have in fact extended over a wide range of food stuffs and also to agricultural raw materials.

The rise in prices has two sides to it. Looked at in one way, it benefits exporting countries, not only in the developed but also the developing world. But when it comes to the harmful effects—the increasingly heavier cost of food for ordinary people—the developing countries are much worse off than the developed. For in the richer nations most people can still afford to pay and their governments can take action to mitigate hardship. In the developing countries, where a much larger part of people's meager incomes goes on food and where governments do not have the resources to subsidize food prices, a rise in the cost of food means real physical suffering for the vast numbers of the poor. No, I am not evoking the specter of widespread deaths from famine. But it is surely already sufficiently chilling to realize that, as a result of privation, many deaths are likely to be hastened.

All in all, it was clear from the beginning of 1973 that the world was heading into the most potentially alarming food situation since the end of the Second World War. . . .

So far [in 1973] we have been fortunate: most crops have

been good, and in some cases very good. But the fact that
the world seems to be overcoming the threat of a full-scale
crisis in the present season up to mid-1974 does not mean
that it has reached safety. It remains extremely disturbing
that at best our prospects for security only extend . . . [for
one year at a time]. . . .

This situation of living from year to year, with many
millions of people subject to the fickleness of the weather
for their basic food supplies, is simply not good enough. If
there is not the international will to solve this basic human
problem, where national interests can only be harmed if it
is *not* solved, then I really wonder what problems the international community is capable of solving.

COSTLY CHOICES [3]

With starvation threatening the planet's poorest inhabitants, nearly unparalleled acts of international cooperation
are needed to prevent the Malthusian nightmare from becoming a reality. Scientific and technological means exist to
feed all the hungry; but the money and the will may not. . . .
The UNs Food and Agriculture Organization . . . [proposes]
stockpiling national grain reserves as a "system of world
food security." FAO officials expect this to ensure "that minimum food supplies are always available to those needing
them on reasonable commercial terms or on grant terms."
Because grain stocks are now so depleted, it will probably
take at least five years to accumulate the 60 to 70 million
tons (enough to feed about 300 million people for one
year) that the FAO estimates the food security system will
require.

The FAO proposal raises several questions that are as yet
unanswered: Who will contribute to the reserve? Who will
finance the storage and transport of the grain and who will
control it? United States Secretary of Agriculture Earl Butz,

[3] From "What to Do: Costly Choices." *Time*. 104:76-80. N. 11, '74. Reprinted
by permission from *Time*, The Weekly Newsmagazine; Copyright Time Inc.

whose views are crucial because no reserve system could function without major US participation, worries that the existence of the surplus stocks could hang over the commercial market and depress the prices paid to farmers for their crops. His fear is based on the government's experience handling the enormous US grain surpluses during the 1950s and 1960s. American farmers commonly—and often bitterly —complain that the government sold some of those stocks whenever grain prices moved up, thus denying farmers a higher return for their investment and work.

If the United States supports the food security system, it will probably insist on ironclad limitations preventing the reserves from being used for anything but emergency relief. Moreover, the United States will want all nations, including the Soviet Union and China, to share in the cost of maintaining the stockpile.

Less controversial is the FAO proposal for a kind of food early warning system, a centralized method for collecting worldwide facts on the types and quantities of crops planted, exports and imports, changes in weather and expected yields. If all nations cooperate—notably including the USSR and China, which treat agricultural information as state secrets—approaching shortages can be spotted early and food-relief missions might avoid the delays that led to thousands of deaths during . . . [the 1973–1974] aid efforts in Ethiopia and the Sahel.

Even though these measures would represent a rare example of international cooperation, they are mere palliatives. They can do no more than rush emergency aid to people once they have begun to hunger. In fact, such aid on a continuous basis could do more harm than good. Donated food often creates "two disincentive effects," notes the University of Chicago's D. Gale Johnson, a leading agricultural economist. It enables the recipient countries to go slow on agricultural development. It also keeps food prices so low in those countries that farmers are reluctant to bring new land under cultivation or invest in machinery, agri-chemicals and modern techniques.

A more lasting remedy would be to encourage nations to adopt more efficient agricultural techniques to increase output. . . . Some of the most necessary are:

Cultivate new lands. Man now farms only half of the earth's 7.8 billion potentially arable acres. Perhaps optimistically, FAO soil technicians reckon that the most promising unused lands are in:

☐ The Amazon River basin of northeast Brazil

☐ The savannahs of Colombia, Venezuela, Ecuador and Brazil, where livestock could graze if plant varieties are bred that would thrive in the high-acid soil

☐ A broad band of 1.7 billion acres across Central Africa now infested with the debilitating tsetse fly

☐ Areas in Malaysia, Thailand, Burma, Indonesia (notably Borneo and Sumatra) and the fertile but politically fragile Mekong River basin

There is almost no virgin land in the world's two most populous nations, India and China. In the United States, farmers are no longer paid to withhold any grain-producing land from cultivation and are tilling a total of 400 million acres. Even though the United States still has 264 million acres that could be farmed, they are now productive as pasture and timberland or are in such poor condition or location that a nearly prohibitive investment would be required to grow crops.

The obstacles are formidable. In the LDCs [Less Developed Countries], as well as the United States, roads must be built to the new lands, irrigation systems installed, warehouses constructed, and the food distribution system expanded and modernized. Because much of the new land is of marginal quality, greater per-acre amounts of water, fertilizer, pesticides and herbicides would be required. Without proper weed killers, for instance, the yield of wheat, rice and corn can drop 20 percent.

One inexpensive and immediate step might be strict land use policies to prevent good farm land from being taken out of production. In the United States 600,000 acres of fertile land are lost each year to the inroads of highways, shopping centers and housing developments. Farmers across the United States have been urging states to enact laws that encourage farmers not to sell their land for nonagricultural use.

Use more fertilizer. Each ton applied to an underdeveloped country's grain crops could increase the harvest by ten tons. Yet the worldwide shortage—expected to last about five more years even for developed nations—has made fertilizer too expensive for LDCs. One immediate answer might be the creation of some kind of fertilizer pool, which has been suggested both by the FAO and United States Secretary of State Henry Kissinger. It would contain fertilizer (or cash to buy fertilizer) contributed by the industrial and oil-possessing states. Needy developing countries could apply to the pool for outright grants of fertilizer or buy it at concessional rates.

The world must also expand its fertilizer productive capacity to meet the expected surge in demand by the end of the century—up at least 300 percent from the current estimated 80 million tons annually. Ideally, many of the new plants should be located in the LDCs. However, the factories cost about $60 million each to build and are complicated to run. Because they use a great amount of energy, some of the plants in India are operating at barely 50 percent of capacity.

Increase the supply of water. From Central America to Asia, the main limit on the wider use of miracle seeds is the lack of water. The FAO estimates that global demand for water will expand 240 percent by the century's end, yet the easiest big dam-and-irrigation projects have already been completed. The only option may be to use available water more efficiently. For example, wheat yields more calories than rice from the same input of water; in terms of water, one pound of beef is 2,500 percent more expensive than one pound of bread.

Improve food distribution and storage. At least one quarter of the world's food disappears between the field and the table. In many LDCs, food is poorly warehoused and is easy prey for rats, insects, fungus and mildew. If the capital were available to upgrade transport systems, build concrete warehouses and modernize marketing methods, there could be a great increase in the food available for underdeveloped countries.

Develop new varieties of crops. Of the nearly 80,000 edible species of plants, only about 50 are cultivated on a large scale. Scientists are trying to do for other grains what the miracle seeds did for wheat and rice. High-lysine corn (a hybrid whose soft kernel contains 66 percent more protein than regular hard-kernel corn) and Triticale (a hybrid of wheat and rye used for livestock feed) are already in limited use. Research is under way in the United States to find high-yield strains of millet, barley and oats and to rearrange leaf configurations on plants to increase their photosynthetic efficiency and allow them to absorb more sunlight.

Development of new foods is a long, tedious process. . . . [In 1973] scientists at Purdue University bred a high-lysine variety of sorghum—but only after working on it for seven years and analyzing ten thousand varieties of the grain. It could be another ten years before that high-protein type will be ready for planting on commercial scale. After the new foods are developed, they sometimes do not satisfy local tastes. For example, residents of India were not satisfied with the soft-kernel, protein-rich, high-lysine corn, preferring their traditionally flinty, hard corn. Cautions economist Johnson: "Even very poor people have their likes and dislikes."

Open agriculture research institutes in the LDCs. A half-century ago, farmers in industrial and underdeveloped nations alike were achieving grain yields of about 900 lbs. per acre; today the LDCs' yield averages 1,100 lbs., versus 1,700 lbs. in the developed nations. "There's no reason—from the standpoint of biology, climate and soils—why yields in the LDCs should not be as high as or higher than those in industrialized countries," says Johnson. The gap can be narrowed by laboratories located in the LDCs that would modify new plant varieties if they are found susceptible to local disease or insects. The labs could also determine which grains grow best in tropical topsoil and develop a soybean that thrives in nontemperate climate zones. Existing research institutes in underdeveloped lands lack money, staff and equipment.

Still other programs could boost food output—but in limited ways. Farmers in the tropics could be taught to plant more than one crop each year (rice in the rainy season, wheat when it is dry). Man could increasingly harvest the ocean for sources of protein. Breeding farms in coastal waters may be especially promising, but will fall far short of filling the world's growing food needs. [See "Fish Farming," in Section III, above.] "People once thought that the resources of the sea were infinite," observes David Wallace of the National Oceanic and Atmospheric Administration. "We now know that these estimates were erroneous." . . .

If the world's food supply were evenly divided among the planet's inhabitants, hunger might be curbed for several decades. But it is not likely that wealthy nations will reduce their living standards to help the LDCs. For example, Americans will not eagerly reduce the 1.3 million tons of fertilizer they spread each year on lawns, golf courses and cemeteries; that amount would produce enough extra grain in the LDCs to feed about 65 million people.

Some nations might be tempted to try emulating China, a country whose name was once synonymous with famine but which is now approaching self-sufficiency in food. The Chinese Communist leadership abolished peasants' private holdings and communalized all plots. Armies of laborers, often under harsh conditions, built irrigation systems, terraced farm lands in mountainous regions, food distribution networks and hundreds of small "backyard" fertilizer factories. All pretense of freedom disappeared, a price (at least in the eyes of the West) that may be too high for most LDCs to pay.

Even the Chinese success is not complete. According to UN estimates, Chinese get only 91 percent of their caloric requirements; a major crop failure could trigger widespread hunger. At best, the Chinese are buying time during which population growth can be checked. Chinese families are encouraged to have no more than two children if they live in the city and three if they live in the countryside.

The number of mouths the world's farmers feed cannot increase indefinitely. Neither unprecedented generosity by the wealthy nations, nor maximum exploitation of known farming techniques, nor anticipated scientific breakthroughs can win what rural economies expert Egbert deVries calls the "stork-farmer race." Unless the experts are underestimating the potential for new discoveries in food production, population control is the *sine qua non* for solving the problem of world hunger. . . .

[Various] programs discussed . . . could at best give the LDCs some more time—but not much—to control their birth rates. To head off still more hunger in the meantime, they will need much help from wealthy nations. Such aid may become quite selective. In the West, there is increasing talk of triage, a commonsense if callous concept that teaches that when resources are scarce, they must be used where they will do most good. (*Triage* is a military term [taken from the French word for selecting or sorting] that describes how limited medical supplies could be allocated on the battlefield. Under triage, first priority is given to the wounded who can make most use of the medicine—those capable of surviving because of treatment but who probably would not survive without it. Those so seriously injured that they cannot be saved have lowest priority.) Thus in the future, if the United States considers building a fertilizer plant or a research lab in a developing country, Washington will more carefully scrutinize what efforts that nation has taken to help itself. If the United States decides that the grant would simply go down the drain as a mere palliative because the recipient country was doing little to improve its food distribution or start a population control program, no help would be sent. This may be a brutal policy, but it is perhaps the only kind that can have any long-range impact. A triage approach could also demand political concessions. The United States may be roundly denounced for "imperialist arrogance," but Washington may feel no obligation to help countries that consistently and strongly opposed it. As Earl Butz told *Time:* "Food is a weapon. It is now one of the principal tools in our negotiating kit."

Even the limited policy of triage, however, may be delayed until it is too late for millions of famished people. "It is going to take a tremendous disaster from famine before people come to grips with the population problem," warns Norman Borlaug, the prime mover of the green revolution. "The stage is set for such a situation right now." Indeed, in parts of Central America, in ten sub-Saharan nations and in some rural areas of India, the twenty-year trend of declining death rates and infant mortality is being reversed. Death rates are rising. This, according to Malthus, is nature's brutal way of redressing the balance when population exceeds food supply—if man himself does not first redress it voluntarily.

A WORLD FOOD POLICY [4]

We may be, literally, one harvest, or one monsoon, away from catastrophe.

A problem of this magnitude requires both immediate and long-range action. Over the longer run people have to be enabled both to feed themselves and to eat better (i.e., improve nutrition). Immediately, however, it is necessary to

[4] From "Feeding the Unfed," by Martin M. McLaughlin, senior fellow, Overseas Development Council. *Commonweal.* 100:376-9. Jl. 12, '74. Reprinted by permission.

feed the hungry. All the complexities of international economic development pale before the stark, clear fact that hungry people have to eat before they can develop. What Pope Paul VI said in *Populorum Progressio* [The Development of Peoples] in 1967 is no less true in 1974: "Today no one can be ignorant any longer of the fact that in whole continents countless men and women are ravished by hunger, countless children are undernourished, so that many of them die in infancy, while the physical growth and mental development of many others are retarded and as a result whole regions are condemned to the most distressing dependency." . . .

It seems essential that the World Food Conference go beyond production and consider distribution (and rural development) as well, i.e., it must move beyond economics, to politics. At this juncture in history, however, the United States does not have a national policy on world food. While we have had a foreign aid program over the years that heavily emphasized agricultural development and have used our food surpluses through PL 480 to help the less developed countries, we have generally shied away from such proposals as a world food bank under international management, to which we would contribute a large share. . . .

Among these private voluntary organizations and many individuals traditionally concerned with the food problem who have been conducting programs among the poor overseas, the conviction has been growing in recent months that there needs to be a broad campaign to remind the American people about this basic problem of hunger and the responsibility of this rich nation to take some leadership in an attack on it. President Lyndon Johnson's . . . initiative for a War on Hunger may be dead, but the problem he addressed remains. There are more hungry people in the developing world now than ever before, and their plight will be made more difficult by the soaring prices of grain and oil—the latter because it is also a basic ingredient of the chemical fertilizers that have made possible the green revolution and the relative gains of the past few years in the poor countries. . . .

In order to get a world food policy adopted by the leaders of this country and pursued vigorously . . . , not only the organizational support of those already in the field, but the moral force of those who have a responsibility to exert such leadership is needed. . . . [An] Overseas Development Council survey . . . clearly indicated that the American people want to help *because it is the right thing to do*—not because of world markets, competition with Communism, or fear that our raw materials will be cut off by the undernourished developing countries. This seems a very encouraging sign; it should also be a warning to legislators and administrators, and a shot in the arm to churchmen and others who are engaged in development education and charitable work.

A world food policy that addresses itself to the problem of hunger is vitally and immediately necessary, but by itself is not enough. People are hungry because they are poor. They are poor because they live in less developed countries or regions, because they do not or are not permitted to share in the fruits of development wherever they live, and because there are too many of them. We have to be concerned about improving the methods of food production and distribution in the developing countries and with getting as many people involved in the solution of their own problems as possible. The answer is not increasing mechanization of farming in the poor countries, but more labor-intensive agriculture that best fits the culture and stage of development of the country. We have evidence that the small, labor-intensive farm may be more efficient in both human and economic terms than the over-mechanized giant; and we have indications that the population growth rate tends to drop as a result of general economic development, rather than as a requisite of it.

Thus the problem of hunger is urging upon us not only the basic duty of charity, the corporal work of mercy, to feed the hungry, but the requirement of justice, which is that of development. As . . . [Pope Paul VI] said in *Populorum Progressio,*

It is not just a matter of eliminating hunger, nor even of reducing poverty. The struggle against destitution, though urgent and necessary, is not enough. It is a question, rather, of building a world where every man, no matter what his race, religion, or nationality, can live a fully human life, freed from servitude imposed on him by other men or natural forces over which he has not sufficient control. . . . This demands great generosity, much sacrifice and unceasing effort on the part of the rich man. . . . Is he prepared to support out of his own pocket works and undertakings organized in favor of the most destitute? Is he ready to pay a higher price for imported goods so that the producer may be more justly rewarded?

Food aid must, in short, be a component of a more generalized development program, based more on improving the quality of life for the individual than on the macro-economic considerations so loved by many of our planners. Development, after all, takes place in people; it is they who are its participants and its subjects, as well as its beneficiaries. . . .

There is a further aspect of this question that should not be ignored in our focus on world hunger. The United States is part of the world, and the poor people of the United States—of whom there is a distressingly large number—are at one with the poor everywhere, even though in dollar terms they don't appear to be. They, too, are poor because they are undeveloped, nonparticipating and numerous. It would be a tragic mistake, a real miscarriage of justice, for us to concentrate so earnestly on the problems abroad that we ignore, or overlook, the injustices in our midst. In the city ghettos, in the rural slums, on the dusty roads of Appalachia, in the small bare rooms where some of the elderly live out their remaining years, we have the same kind of grinding poverty and crushing inhumanity as in the favelas and barrios of Latin America and the rat-infested hovels of Calcutta. A world food policy must include a food (and development) policy for this country as well. . . .

This country has been favored with an unprecedentedly high material standard of living; to a considerable extent it has been earned by hard work, but to a large degree it has also resulted from good fortune. We should not pretend that we are better than others, though we are luckier; and we cannot pretend that it is right for 6 percent of the world's population to consume, even partially waste, nearly half of the world's product every year. "Development," said Pope Paul VI, "is the new name for peace." It is not a matter of charity, but of justice, for, as everyone knows, peace is the fruit of justice.

A BOLD PLAN [5]

Martin Luther King had a dream that still echoes in the conscience of America. I have a plan that will, I hope, reverberate as insistently in our minds. It concerns feeding —reasonably—the people of the world, poor and affluent alike. . . .

We have begun to face some of the fundamental answers to . . . questions of human survival. In essence these are the control of waste by the affluent and the control of population by all. The affluent must learn to simplify their diet by reducing their consumption of livestock and livestock products, and by substituting vegetable proteins for some of their animal proteins. There are four good reasons for doing this. The most personally compelling is the fact that medical authorities are increasingly discovering that too much consumption of animal products and proteins is dangerous to health. (Evidence already indicates that excessive meat-eating increases the likelihood of both heart disease and cancer.) An additional argument—increasingly convincing to

[5] From "I Have a Plan," by Orville Freeman, former U.S. Secretary of Agriculture and chief executive officer, Business International Corporation. *Saturday Review*. 2:12-14+. D. 14, '74. Reprinted by permission.

many people even in the affluent societies—is that meat
is more expensive than other, equally nutritious, forms of
food. Also, the production of animal proteins is more demanding on the ecology of our planet than are simpler diets.
And finally, there is the moral imperative at this stage of
human evolution, which demands that the affluent stop
literally taking food out of the mouths of the poor. In a
world of scarcity—the world we now have and will have for
some time to come—the arithmetic of consumption is fright-
fully simple. If some of us consume more, others must of
necessity consume less. Inevitably those who consume less
are the world's poor, who have no remaining notches left
with which to tighten their belts.

What the world's poor must learn, along with the rich—
and the rich must help to make it possible—is that there is
no security in a large family. It is quite clear that the world
cannot continue on its present demographic path. Future
population growth will be reduced either because of rising
death rates (a phenomenon appearing already in some developing countries) or because of declining birth rates. The
choice is finally very simple: It is between famine and family planning.

Whatever kind of dust nationalistic pride and prejudice
still throws in people's eyes, the real need for all is for a
worldwide effort, stepped up sharply and immediately, to
stabilize the world's population. What we need is zero
growth everywhere—and as soon as possible.

To achieve this goal, a four-part package is required. It
consists of: (1) family-planning services made available to
everyone; (2) meeting the basic economic and social needs
of the poor so that they lose the motivation that drives them
to create large families; (3) new roles for women that make
it possible for half the world's population to achieve social
status and self-fulfillment through activities other than bear-
ing and rearing offspring; (4) devising national economic
and social policies that encourage and promote low fertility
instead of propagating population explosions, which spell

tragedy for the family, insurmountable problems for the nation, and disaster for the world. That all of this can be done has already been demonstrated by societies as different in size, economic policy, and political principle as Singapore on one side of the spectrum and the People's Republic of China on the other.

However, even if we start a plan for action now to control waste and population, it will take decades before these fundamental efforts achieve the required results. Meanwhile the world must be fed. I have a plan that could do it.

A Plan for Action Now

The plan calls for a global effort with three ingredients: resources, know-how, policies.

Resources. In the area of resources the world still has vast stretches of land that have never been put to the plow but could be, and yields on currently producing acres in the developing countries could be doubled and tripled if modern techniques were used. I have, for example, recently returned from Zambia. There I was shown land, about as large as Texas, that has never been cultivated. I do not know exactly what the water problems are. But in one enormous experimental farm, it was demonstrated convincingly that if there is a water problem, it can be solved. How many other millions of acres exist in Africa that have never been used?

In Asia, on the Indian subcontinent, the Ganges delta alone is as large, and could be made as fertile, as the entire Midwest cornbelt of the United States. In Brazil, and in tropical countries around the globe, the right inputs would make possible double and even triple cropping where now there is either nothing or at least stick agriculture.

What is true for food is true also for fertilizer. The developing world is replete with natural gas that goes unused. In some places it has never been tapped. In others, such as the Middle East, it is being wasted—flared off at oil wellheads. With the right technology, it could be converted into inexpensive fertilizer, which the countries that need it most can afford. . . .

Know-How. It takes know-how. And the know-how is available. What needs to be designed is a system that will bring together the land, the know-how, and the capital required for creating a productive enterprise. I think I can suggest a system that would work and would serve two additional purposes important to the economic health and social welfare of the world, that is, the creation of jobs in the developing countries that are plagued by unemployment and underemployment, and the introduction into the market economy of segments of the population that now struggle along on a bare subsistence level.

My system starts with the fact that the change in oil prices has brought about an enormous concentration of capital that cannot be put to use in the countries accumulating it. They must put it somewhere and are under increasing pressure from the whole world, and particularly from the "superpoor"—the developing countries that have no quickly marketable natural resources—to use at least some of it to help people now threatened by famine as the direct result of the dizzying cost-climb of oil and all the products derived from it.

The second component of the system is the array of major international agribusiness firms that have the experience, the technology, and the management know-how to put to use some of the vast acreage that now lies idle or is cultivated in inefficient, outmoded ways. In establishing productive, large-scale farming ventures, these companies could provide supervisory and technical services to hundreds of nearby small farmers, who could become contract suppliers. Satellite farming systems of this type are already quite widespread in such agricultural sectors as sugar, vegetables, poultry, and a range of exotic products including bananas and cashew nuts. Utilized in this manner, the capital for the required inputs—fertilizer, chemicals, and seed; the know-how and organizational skill for applying modern agricultural technology effectively; and the processing and marketing ability that can get the food where it is needed and at the same time provide a decent living standard for the producer—can all be brought together.

Policies. If this system has the ring of a "do-gooder" scheme, the ring is one of pure gold. The fact is that well-run agribusiness projects in some developing countries have returned as much as 30 percent a year on investment. Oil-producer money looking for a home can hardly do better. And aggressive, imaginative international companies always respond to an opportunity that makes profitable use of their abilities.

What the system requires as a third input—and that, I suspect, will turn out to be the most problematic component —is sensible, constructive policies from the political leaders of the developing countries. Such policies are hard to come by. Agriculture is complex and expensive, and demonstrable results with a clear political payoff take time to achieve. Effective political pressure to build up agriculture is the exception, rather than the rule, in the developing world. Where it does exist, it tends to come from an entrenched, feudal, land-owning elite, which is, in today's world, more of a political liability than an asset. Small farmers are seldom, if ever, organized. The temptation to pay lip service to agriculture instead of moving to action—particularly to the complicated and sometimes politically hazardous action of getting modern agricultural technology adjusted to a labor-intensive basis reaching the small producer—is very great. But action is clearly needed and, I believe, unavoidable. If the right policies are pursued, I am convinced that the capital and technology will be forthcoming.

The Institutional Framework

While this tripartite system is put into place on the production side, parallel work must be done on building the institutions that will support and sustain the productive effort over the long pull.

In constructing these institutions, the most immediate task is to shore up the crumbling roof that threatens to crash down on a segment of mankind. *A global commitment is necessary for preventing large-scale famine in 1975.* The industrialized countries and those of the oil- and cash-rich OPEC (Organization of Petroleum-Exporting Countries) must make the major contributions to this effort, but all the more fortunate countries of the world that have been spared harvest failures should play their part.

However such a program of relief is financed, it is clear that the biggest share of the needed grains must come from the North American continent, although both the USSR and Europe seem to have some reserves that can be tapped for this emergency. In this food-short world, there will inevitably be upward pressure on prices, and that will work a hardship on consumers in the producing countries as well as on the countries needing the grain. We thus face a great, immediate challenge in institution-building, and as in most institutions, this fundamental challenge is a moral one. It is simply whether the more fortunate world is going to feed other nations, even at the expense of higher food costs at home, or turn its back on the hungry of the world.

Once this shoring up has been accomplished, the walls of the institutional edifice must be strengthened. This means that *we must move toward the orderly marketing of agricultural products on a worldwide basis,* starting with an ongoing exchange of information and the planning of reserve management. This would avoid go-it-alone moves, such as the USSR's secret manipulation of the wheat market in 1972 or the United States' sudden export embargo on soya in 1973, both of which sent shock waves through the entire world, with economic and political reverberations that are still being felt.

Finally, *the world must design commodity arrangements that work.* It could be done quite simply. . . . The main requirement is to create an international body that would set minimum and maximum prices for each basic agricultural commodity. If prices drop below the established minimum because of an exceptionally good crop year, governments could buy the staple in question and use it to build reserves. Such reserves would be completely insulated from the market, unless and until prices soared to the established maximum level—as they did in 1973–74, when a production shortfall of 3 percent resulted in a price hike of 250 percent. With such parameters of safety and sanity established, the free world market could function as it does now to fix prices and allocate resources. . . .

In my judgment, nothing novel or radical is needed in the way of institutions that could serve the interim purpose. A strengthened, widened GATT (General Agreement on Tariffs and Trade) would suffice. GATT's concern in the past (and it has done well by that concern) has been to assure equitable access to markets. This concern should now be widened to include equitable access to supplies. The United States has provided the leadership that moved the nations of the developed world—the old rich—toward progressively opening their markets. Similar leadership should now persuade the countries with the vital raw materials— the new rich—to move in the same direction in offering fair and equitable access to supplies.

Of all supplies, food is the most fundamental. It is my belief that if the world can get together to find a solution to the problem of food, solutions to other supply problems will follow. And it is my conviction that the answer to the problems of interdependence is not a scurrying for cover behind national barriers, but more interdependence, the construction of institutions and relationships that build on sense and sensibility by all, for all.

Where food is concerned, we know only too well what the problems are. They are staring us in the face. Let us not dissect them to distraction or despair at their magnitude. Solutions exist. My plan is one. Let us move to apply them.

BIBLIOGRAPHY

An asterisk (*) preceding a reference indicates that the article or a part of it has been reprinted in this book.

BOOKS, PAMPHLETS, AND DOCUMENTS

*American Freedom from Hunger Foundation. The American Freedom from Hunger Foundation. The Foundation. 1100 17th St. N.W. Washington, D.C. 20036. '74.

American Freedom from Hunger Foundation. Readings on world hunger. The Foundation. 1100 17th St. N.W. Washington, D.C. 20036. '75. mimeo.

Bard, R. L. Food aid and international agricultural trade; a study in legal and administrative control. Heath. '72.

Blakeslee, L. L. and others. World food production, demand, and trade. Iowa State University Press. '73.

Borgstrom, G. A. Focal points; a global food strategy. Macmillan. '73.

Borgstrom, G. A. Harvesting the earth. INTEXT. '73.

Borgstrom, G. A. The hungry planet; the modern world at the edge of famine. 2d rev. ed. Macmillan. '72.

Brown, L. R. and Eckholm, E. P. By bread alone. Praeger. '74.

Brown, L. R. and Eckholm, E. P. Our dietary habits: should they be changed? for what reasons? (Vital Issues, v 24, no 2). Center for Information on America. Washington, Conn. 06793. '74.

CARE. World Hunger Fund Report no 1. CARE, Inc. 660 First Ave. New York 10016. '75.

CARE. World of CARE. CARE, Inc. 660 First Ave. New York 10016. '73.

Citizens' Board of Inquiry into Hunger and Malnutrition in the United States. Hunger U.S.A. revisited: a report. Southern Regional Council. 52 Fairlie St. N.W. Atlanta, Ga. 30303. '72. Published in cooperation with the National Council on Hunger and Malnutrition.

Clark, F. L. and Pirie, N. W. eds. Four thousand million mouths; scientific humanism and the shadow of world hunger. Books for Libraries Press. '70.

Cochrane, W. W. Feast or famine; the uncertain world of food and agriculture and its policy implications for the United States. (Report no 136) National Planning Association. 1606 New Hampshire Ave. N.W. Washington, D.C. 20009. '74.

Cochrane, W. W. World food problem; a guardedly optimistic view. Crowell. '69.

Feeding the world's hungry: the challenge to business. Continental Bank. Public Affairs Division. 231 S. La Salle St. Chicago 60693. '75. mimeo. (Transcript of international conference)

Food and Agriculture Organization of the United Nations. FAO in 1974. The Organization. Rome. '75.

*Food and Agriculture Organization of the United Nations. FAO: what it is, what it does, how it works. The Organization. Rome. '74.

Food and Agriculture Organization of the United Nations. Things to come: the world food crisis—way out. The Organization. Rome. '74.

Franda, M. F. Food research in India. (South Asia Series. v 18, no 9) American Universities Field Staff, Inc. P.O. Box 150. Hanover, N.H. 03755. '74.

Franda, M. F. India: "an unprecedented national crisis." (South Asia Series. v 17, no 5) American Universities Field Staff, Inc. P.O. Box 150. Hanover, N.H. 03755. '73.

Gardner, R. N. World food and energy crisis: the role of international organizations; report of conference held May 1974 at the United Nations and Rensselaerville, N.Y. Institute on Man and Science. Rensselaerville, N.Y. 12147. '74.

*Goffio, F. L. Twenty-eighth annual report, CARE, Inc., 1974. CARE, Inc. 660 First Ave. New York 10016. '74.

*Hakel, M. D. ed. Between you and hunger; report of Midwest conference on food policy, June 6-7, 1974. Minnesota Farmers Union. 1275 University Ave. St. Paul, Minn. 55104. '74.
    Reprinted in this book: address by L. R. Brown. p 32-4.

Hakel, M. D. ed. Food: today, tomorrow—and then what? special report on the United Nations World food conference. Minnesota Farmers Union. 1275 University Ave. St. Paul, Minn. 55104. '74.

Halacy, D. S. Feast and famine. Macrae Smith. '71.

Halacy, D. S. The geometry of hunger. Harper. '72.

Hanna, W. A. Singapore: food. (Southeast Asia Series. v 22, no 12) American Universities Field Staff, Inc. P.O. Box 150. Hanover, N.H. 03755. '74.

Hathaway, D. E. World food situation: how serious is it? (Vital Issues. v 23, no 9) Center for Information on America. Washington, Conn. 06793. '74.

Heilbroner, Robert. An inquiry into the human prospect. Norton. '74.

*Hewitt, W. A. Address before conference on Famine, 1975? at Dartmouth College, February 18, 1975. Dartmouth College. Department of Geography. Hanover, N.H. 03755. '75. mimeo.

Hollings, E. F. The case against hunger; a demand for a national policy. Cowles. '70.

*Huke, R. E. One view of the world in the year 2000; address at workshop organized by Wright-Ingraham Institute at La Paz, Mexico, January 14-17, 1975. The Author. Dartmouth College. Department of Geography. Hanover, N.H. 03755. '75.

Katz, Robert. A giant in the earth. Stein & Day. '73.

McLin, Jon. Western Europe and the world food problem. (West Europe Series. v 9, no 6) American Universities Field Staff, Inc. P.O. Box 150. Hanover, N.H. 03755. '74.

*Malthus, T. R. On population, ed. & introd. by Gertrude Himmelfarb. (Modern Library) Random House. '60.

Paddock, William and Paddock, Paul. Famine—1975! America's decision: who will survive? Little. '67.

Poleman, T. T. and Freebairn, D. K. eds. Food, population, and employment; the impact of the green revolution. Praeger. '73.

Ravenholt, Albert. So many makes for malnutrition. (Southeast Asia Series. v 22, no 5) American Universities Field Staff, Inc. P.O. Box 150. Hanover, N.H. 03755. '74.

Simon, Paul and Simon, Arthur. The politics of world hunger; grass-roots politics and world poverty. Harper's Magazine Press. '73.

*Snow, C. P. State of siege. Scribner. '69.
    Also included in: Public affairs, by C. P. Snow. Scribner. '71.

Stewart, M. S. Food for the world's hungry. (Public Affairs Pamphlet no 511) Public Affairs Committee. 381 Park Ave. New York 10016. '74.

United States. Agency for International Development. Catalog of selected AID publications. The Agency. Washington, D.C. 20523. '74.

United States. Congress. House. U.S. policy and world food needs; hearings before the Subcommittee on International Organizations and Movements and on Foreign Economic Policy of the Committee on Foreign Affairs, September 10-12, 1974. 93d Congress; 2d Session. Supt. of Docs. Washington, D.C. 20402. '74.

United States. Congress. House. Committee on Agriculture. Subcommittee on Department Operations. Malthus and America: a report about food and people. 93d Congress; 2d Session. Supt. of Docs. Washington, D.C. 20402. '74.

United States. Congress. House. Committee on Foreign Affairs. Report of the special mission to Europe, November 6-17, 1974: I, World Food Conference (p 1-6). 93d Congress; 2d Session. Supt. of Docs. Washington, D.C. 20402. '74.

*United States. Congress. House. Committee on Foreign Affairs. Report on the World Food Conference, November 26, 1974. 93d Congress; 2d Session. Supt. of Docs. Washington, D.C. 20402. '74.

United States. Congress. Senate. Select Committee on Nutrition and Human Needs. Emergency food and medical services. 93d Congress; 1st Session. Supt. of Docs. Washington, D.C. 20402. '73.

United States. Congress. Senate. Select Committee on Nutrition and Human Needs. Hunger—1973. 93d Congress; 1st Session. Supt. of Docs. Washington, D.C. 20402. '73.

United States. Congress. Senate. Select Committee on Nutrition and Human Needs. Numerous hearings and reports on world food situation. 93d Congress; 2d Session. Supt. of Docs. Washington, D.C. 20402. '74.

United States. Congress. Senate. Select Committee on Nutrition and Human Needs. Report on nutrition and the international situation. 93d Congress; 2d Session. Supt. of Docs. Washington, D.C. 20402. '74.
    Bibliography: p 55-7.

*United States. Department of Agriculture. Economic Research Service. Summary of the world food situation and prospects to 1985. (Foreign Agricultural Economic Report no 98) U.S. Department of Agriculture. Economic Research Service. Washington, D.C. 20250. '75.

United States. Department of Agriculture. Office of Communication. List of available publications of the United States Department of Agriculture; M. W. Johnson, comp. (List no 11). The Department. Washington, D.C. 20250. '73.

United States. Department of Agriculture. Office of Communication. Real facts about food. The Department. Washington, D.C. 20250. '74.

United States. General Accounting Office. Increasing world food supplies—crisis and challenge; Department of State and other agencies: report to the Congress by the Comptroller General of the United States. (B-159652) The Office. 441 G St. N.W. Washington, D.C. 20548. '74.

United States. Office of the President. 1973 annual report on public law 480. (House Document no 93-362) 93d Congress; 2d Session. Supt. of Docs. Washington, D.C. 20402. '74.

Waterbury, John. 'Aish: Egypt's growing food crisis. (Northeast Africa Series, v 19, no 3) American Universities Field Staff, Inc. P.O. Box 150. Hanover, N.H. 03755. '74.

PERIODICALS

Africa Report. 18:6-13. Jl. '73. Creeping catastrophe. J. E. Rosenthal.

*America. 131:67-9. Ag. 24, '74. The Sahel: tragedy of underdevelopment, V. S. Kearney.

America. 131:70-2. Ag. 24, '74. Three billion meals a day. E. J. Cripps.

America. 132:144-6. Mr. 1, '75. System in crisis: Rome food conference. J. V. Blewett.

America. 132:146-9. Mr. 1, '75. Persistent species of Rome: NGO's [nongovernmental organizations]. H. A. Jack.

American Federationist. 80:18-22. My. '73. Providing the world with enough food. J. B. Cordaro.

American Journal of Agricultural Economics. 55:778-90. D. '73. Conflicts and consistencies in the agricultural policies of the United States and Canada. G. E. Brandon.

Americas. 25:S1-15. Ap. '73. Agriculture and development. C. J. Molestina Escudero and G. de Zéndegui.

Annals of the American Academy of Political and Social Science. 405:65-74. Ja. '73. Impact of urbanization on agricultural processes. G. F. Winfield.

Annals of the Association of American Geographers. 63:319-30. S. '73. Green revolution in India. A. K. Chakravarti.

Atlantic. 232:85-90. S. '73. Farming and mining; there is no land to spare. H. M. Caudill.
Same with title: Farming versus strip-mining. Current. 156:37-45. N. '73.
Same abridged with title: Can we survive strip mining? Reader's Digest. 103:65-9. D. '73.

Atlantic. 233:98-105. My. '74. Making of the sub-Saharan wasteland. Claire Sterling.
Same abridged with title: Death stalks the Sahel. Reader's Digest. 104:80-4. Je. '74.

BioScience. 24:216-24. Ap. '74. Maximum production capacity of food crops. S. H. Wittwer.

BioScience. 24:499-504. S. '74. Ocean's food web, a changing paradigm. L. R. Pomeroy.

*BioScience. 24:561-8. O. '74. Living on a lifeboat. Garrett Hardin.
Same abridged with title: Lifeboat ethics; the case against helping the poor. Psychology Today. bibliog. (p 140) 8:38+. S. '74; Discussion. 8:7-12. D. '74.

BioScience. 25:131-3. F. '75. World food conference—a frustrating first step. G. W. Thomas.

Bulletin of the Atomic Scientists. 29:50-4. O. '73. Nutrition crunch: a world view. David Spurgeon.

Business Horizons. 17:5-14. D. '74. Arab petroleum = American food. Wayne Bartholomew and G. A. Wing.

Business Week. p 62-6+. Ap. 28, '73. Agriculture; biggest growth
    industry in the U.S.
Challenge. 17:48-53. Mr./Ap. '74. Food shortage is not inevitable.
    E. P. Reubens.
Challenge. 17:12-24. S./O. '74. Food and hunger: the balance sheet.
    L. R. Brown and E. P. Eckholm.
Christian Century. 90:797-8. Ag. 15, '73. African famine and be-
    yond.
Christian Century. 91:870-1. S. 25, '74. Hunger: domestic and
    global links. Arthur Simon.
Christian Century. 92:60-3. Ja. 22, '75. Hunger exercise [experienc-
    ing what hunger feels like]. R. A. Hoehn.
Christian Science Monitor. Sec. II, p 5. Ja. 22, '75. How to help
    world hunger. Lynde McCormick.
Christianity Today. 17:42-4. S. 14, '73. Tragedy in Timbuktu:
    Africa's creeping calamity. Barrie Doyle.
Christianity Today. 18:48-50. Ap. 12, '74. Famine in Africa: it's
    worse. Barrie Doyle.
Commentary. 58:25-9. Jl. '74. Against the Neo-Malthusians. B.
    Bruce-Briggs.
*Commonweal. 99:457-9. F. 8, '74. The world food problem. F. M.
    Lappe.
        First appeared in Hastings Center Report. Institute of Society, Ethics and
        the Life Sciences. Hastings-on-Hudson, N.Y. 10706.
Commonweal. 99:460-3. F. 8, '74. Politics of hunger. R. J. Neu-
    haus.
Commonweal. 99:523-4. Mr. 1, '74. Silent crisis: food for the poor
    at high prices.
Commonweal. 100:374-5. Jl. 12, '74. Food crisis. Arthur Simon.
*Commonweal. 100:376-9. Jl. 12, '74. Feeding the unfed. M. M.
    McLaughlin.
        Condensed with title: Needed: a world food policy. Current. 165:15-20. S.
        '74.
Conference Board Record. 11:17-20. Jl. '74. Ending the tyranny of
    hunger. R. E. Anderson.
Congressional Digest. 53:291-314. D. '74. Question of increasing
    controls over U.S. food exports.
Congressional Quarterly Weekly Report. 33:160-1. Ja. 18, '75.
    Food aid abroad: should U.S. give more?
Current. 148:3-5. F. '73. How to feed the poor? John Kramer.
Current. 160:42-50. Mr. '74. Toward zero-growth or disaster? Roger
    Revelle.
Current History. 65:120-3+. S. '73. Food and agricultural prob-
    lems in China. C. Y. Cheng.
Department of State Bulletin. 71:821-9. D. 16, '74. World food

conference meets at Rome; address, November 5, 1974. H. A. Kissinger.

Department of State Bulletin. 71:829-31. D. 16, '74. World food conference meets at Rome; address, November 6, 1974. E. L. Butz.

Ebony. 29:35-8+. N. '73. Death stalks West Africa. C. T. Rowan.

*Ecologist. 3:334-7. S. '73. Will the desert bloom? Peter Bunyard.

*Economic Geography. 50:47-58. Ja. '74. San Bartolome and the green revolution. R. E. Huke.

*Economic Leaflets (University of Florida. Bureau of Economic and Business Research). 31:1-4. Ag.-S. '72. Promises and problems of the green revolution. C. N. Smith.

Economist. 250:63-4. F. 2, '74. What to do about food prices.

Economist. 251:43-4+. Ap. 20, '74. Next harvest.

Economist. 253:19-20+. N. 2, '74. Fat years and the lean. Barbara Ward.

Environment. 14:10-15. D. '72. Big farm. M. J. Perelman and K. P. Shea.

Environment. 15:12-17. Mr. '73. End to chemical farming? Duane Chapman.

Environment. 15:3+. Je. '73. Meat and the environment. D. H. Kohl.

European Community. p 3-5. N. '74. Fighting world hunger: Community joins in World food conference. Vincent Roberts.

Farm Journal. 97:24-5. D. '73. World's worries over food. Lane Palmer.

Farm Journal. 98:20-1+. D. '74. Famine: the world wants you to solve it.

Farm Journal. 99:A1. F. '75. What you can do to help the hungry. Laura Lane.

*Farm Journal. 99:32-3+. F. '75. Real answer to starvation. R. C. Black.

First National City Bank Monthly Economic Letter. p 5-7. O. '74. Food: the costly trip from farm to table.

Focus. 23:1-8. Ja. '73. India's agriculture. A. K. Chakravarti.

Forbes. 111:32-4+. Mr. 15, '73. Can agriculture save the dollar?

Forbes. 115:15. F. 1, '75. Hello, sucker! [investing in dehydrated food]

Foreign Affairs. 52:511-37. Ap. '74. World food: prices and the poor. L. P. Schertz.

*Foreign Affairs. 53:98-120. O. '74. Coping with famine. Jean Mayer.

*Fortune. 89:84-9+. F. '74. We can't take food for granted anymore. L. A. Mayer.

Fortune. 89:90-5+. F. '74. Ominous changes in the world's weather. Tom Alexander.

Fortune. 91:61-2. Ja. '75. Humane intentions, cruel consequences.

Futurist. 8:56-64. Ap. '74. Global food insecurity. L. R. Brown.

*Futurist. 8:65-7. Ap. '74. Solving the world's food problem. A. H. Boerma.

Futurist. 8:169-78. Ag. '74. Coming world struggle for food. G. T. T. Molitor.

*Geographical Magazine. 45:734-9. Jl. '73. Rural revolution. David Grigg.

Harper's Magazine. 247:3-10+. Jl. '73. Food: the spirit made flesh; symposium. Tony Jones.

Harper's Magazine. 248:16-18+. F. '74. Helping hand behind food prices. R. L. Miller.
  Reply with rejoinder. Harper's Magazine. 248:102. Ap. '74. R. E. LeMoine.

Harper's Magazine. 248:15-16. Je. '74. Scourge of famine. Timothy Dickinson.

Harper's Magazine. 248:16+. Je. '74. Strangulation in the open air. Richard Selzer.

Hunger (Canada). 2:19-21. Spring/Summer '73. World food shortage. A. H. Boerma.

Institutions/Volume Feeding Management. 72:front cover+. Je. 1, '73. Food crisis 1973: a special issue.

Journal of Economic History. 33:274-90. Mr. '73. Corporate farming in the United States. P. M. Raup.

Middle East Journal. 28:381-95. Autumn '74. Population, food and agriculture in the Arab countries. E. H. Tuma.

Monthly Bulletin of Agricultural Economics and Statistics (FAO). 23:1-13. S. '74. Population, food supply and agricultural development.

Monthly Review (Federal Reserve Bank of Kansas City). p 12-19. D. '74. 1975 agricultural outlook: a year of continuing adjustment.

Ms. 3:54-5+. Ja. '75. Let them eat hamburger: relationship of world food supply to U.S. government agricultural policy. Emma Rothschild.

Nation. 217:207-11. S. 10, '73. New world food crisis: the sputtering green revolution. Richard Critchfield.

Nation. 217:366-71. O. 15, '73. Latin America's tragedy: illusion of agrarian reform. Penny Lemoux.

Nation. 217:456-62. N. 5, '73. Good climate for agribusiness. G. L. Baker.

*Nation. 220:197-200. F. 22, '75. Famine in Africa; no act of God. A. M. Warhaftig.

National Observer. p 1+. Mr. 29, '75. Let 'em starve. M. T. Malloy.

Nation's Business. 61:28-32. Je. '73. Earl Butz: plowing new furrows for U.S. agriculture.

Nation's Business. 63:26-9. F. '75. Can we produce enough food? H. E. Talmadge.

Natural History. 82:20-2. Mr. '73. Withering green revolution. Marvin Harris.

Natural History. 82:28-9+. O. '73. New ways to increase man's food: photorespiration experiments. A. W. Galston.

New Republic. 170:14-17. Mr. 23, '74. Helping the poorest of the poor. Richard Critchfield.

New Republic. 170:11-12. Ap. 6, '74. Famine. R. W. Dietsch.

New Republic. 170:16-19. Je. 15. '74. India: the lost years. Richard Critchfield.

New Republic. 171:5-7. Jl. 6, '74. Feeding a hungry world.

New Statesman. 86:681-2. N. 9, '73. Wiping famine off the map. John Maddox.

New York Times. p 1+. O. 6, '74. Malnutrition is up sharply among world's children. H. M. Schmeck, Jr.

New York Times. p 1. N. 17, '74. Food conference, in last day, forms new U. N. agency. William Robbins.

New York Times. p 4. N. 19, '74. Food parley: plans laid for future action. William Robbins.

New York Times. Sec IV, p 85-6. Ja. 25, '75. Hungry world struggles for more food. David Bird.

New York Times. p 20. Ap. 27, '75. U. N. food agency, despite some successes, is beset by uncertainties and conflicts. Paul Hofmann.

*New York Times. p 34. Je. 3, '75. Food experts see several countries in greater peril of hunger and possible starvation than last year. Boyce Rensberger.

New York Times Magazine. p 10-11+. Ja. 6, '74. Fat Americans. R. F. Spark.

New York Times Magazine. p 9-11. Ja. 5, '75. Triage: who shall be fed? who shall starve? Wade Greene.

*New York Times Magazine. p 15+. Ap. 27, '75. Green revolution lives. Alan Anderson, Jr.

New Yorker. 51:40-4+. My. 26, '75. A reporter at large: short term, long term [United Nations World Food Conference, Rome, November 1974]. Emma Rothschild.

Newsweek. 83:40-1. Ap. 1, '74. Running out of food?

Newsweek. 84:46+. N. 4, '74. Great famine.

Newsweek. 84:56-60. N. 11, '74. Running out of food? [special report]

Newsweek. 84:13. D. 23. '74. Island of plenty. J. G. Montgomery.

Nutrition Review. 32:97-104. Ap. 74. Nutrition and numbers in the third world. J. G. Harrar.

Organic Gardening and Farming. 20:60-3. Jl. '73. Coming revolution in agricultural research. Jerome Goldstein.

Organic Gardening and Farming. 21:30-4. S. '74. Famine in America is possible. Robert Rodale.

Parents Magazine & Better Homemaking. 50:17+. Mr. '75. Can we solve the world-wide food crisis? H. R. Labouisse.

Progressive. 39:13-17. Ja. '75. Food monopolies. Daniel Zwerdling.

Progressive. 39:18-19. Ja. '75. Exporting food monopolies. D. J. Balz.

Ramparts. 11:16-20+. Je. '73. Chilean experiment: revolution in the countryside? José Yglesias.

Ramparts. 11:33-5+. Je. '73. Vegetarian manifesto. F. M. Lappé.

Ramparts. 13:29-32+. S. '74. Feast or famine: the choices for mankind. Terence McCarthy.

Reader's Digest. 102:146-50. Ap. '73. Why the Soviet Union can't feed itself. Edward Hughes.

Redbook. 144:33-4+. Mr. '75. How we can help the world's hungry people. Margaret Mead.

Saturday Evening Post. 246:116-20+. Ap. '74. Great American food revolution. W. B. Furlong.

Saturday Evening Post. 246:54-5+. N. '74. Give us this day our daily bread. Alan Kimbell.

*Saturday Review. 2:12-14+. D. 14, '74. I have a plan. Orville Freeman.

Saturday Review. 2:63-4. Ja. 11. '75. World food conference: strong goals, weak commitment. P. W. Quigg.

*Saturday Review. 2:4. Mr. 8, '75. Of life and lifeboats. Norman Cousins.

Saturday Review/World. 1:12-15. O. 9, '73. Europe's farm muddle: common agricultural policy of the Common market. R. C. Longworth.

Saturday Review/World. 1:14-16+. D. 18, '73. What happened to America the beneficent? S. S. Rosenfeld.

Science. 181:634-8. Ag. 17, '73. World food situation; pessimism comes back into vogue. Nicholas Wade.
  Reply. Science. 183:26+. Ja. 11, '74. W. H. Pawley.

Science. 182:121-5. O. 12, '73. Power, fresh water, and food from cold, deep sea water. D. F. Othmer and O. A. Roels.

Science. 182:1321-3. D. 28, '73. Agriculture: rise to prominence at home and abroad. Nicholas Wade.

Science. 183:1175-6. Mr. 22 '74. U.S.-U.S.S.R. detente: bumpy progress on the agricultural front. Nicholas Wade.

Science 184:307-16. Ap. 19, '74. Energy use in the U.S. food system. J. S. Steinhart and C. E. Steinhart.

Science. 184:548-50. My. 3, '74. Food and nutrition: is America due for a national policy? Constance Holden.

Science. 185:680-2. Ag. 23, '74. Lester Brown: tireless sounder of the world alert. Constance Holden.

Science. 185:844-5. S. 6, '74. Green revolution: creators still quite hopeful on world food. Nicholas Wade.

Science. 186:877-81. D. 6, '74. World climates and food supply variations. J. E. Newman and R. C. Pickett.

Science. 186:1093-6. D. 20, '74. Green revolution (I): a just technology, often unjust in use. Nicholas Wade.

Science. 186:1186-9+. D. 27, '74. Green revolution (II): problems of adapting a western technology. Nicholas Wade.

Science. 188:501-55. My. 9, '75. Food: economics, politics and social structure; symposium; with editorial comment.

Science News. 104:42-3. Jl. 21, '73. Green revolution: phase 2. Joan Arehart-Treichel.

*Science News. 105:306-8. My. 11, '74. Omens of famine. J. H. Douglas.

*Science News. 105:322-3. My. 18, '74. Confronting famine. J. H. Douglas.

Science News. 106:53-4. Jl. 27, '74. Famine fears rise, battle lines form.

Scientific American. 231:26,160-70. S. '74. Food and population: with biographical sketch. Roger Revelle.

Sea Frontiers. 20:158-71,190-1. My. '74. United Nations fishes the Caribbean; with biographical sketch. C. P. Idyll.

Senior Scholastic. 104:19-21. Mr. 28, '74. What's happening down on the farm?

Senior Scholastic. 105:6-11. O. 24, '74. How bad is the global food crisis?

Senior Scholastic. 105:12-13. O. 24, '74. Great famines.

Senior Scholastic. 105:14-15. O. 24, '74. Should we cut down on meat to save our grain supplies?

Successful Farming. 71:27-37. N. '73. Agriculture's new era: off and running; views of 37 experts.

Successful Farming. 73:4 Ja. '75. Viewpoint on the world food crisis.

Technology Review. 77:12-19. D. '74. World-wide confrontation of population and food supply. N. S. Scrimshaw.

Technology Review. 77:20-9. D. '74. Technological change in the food industry. G. F. Bloom and R. C. Curhan.

Technology Review. 77:40-5. D. '74. Earth's climatic history. R. E. Newell.

Technology Review. 77:33-9. Ja. '75. Desert food factories. C. N. Hodges.

*Time. 104:66-8+. N. 11, '74. World food crisis.

UN Monthly Chronicle. 11:29-33. Mr. '74. World food conference; excerpts from address, February 11, 1974. S. A. Marei.

U.S. News & World Report. 74:74-6. Mr. 5, '73. Asia's trouble returns: too many babies, too little food.

U.S. News & World Report. 76:50-2. Ja. 28, '74. Formula for world famine? [energy gap + population explosion + droughts]

U.S. News & World Report. 76:52-3. Mr. 18, '74. Why grocery bills around the world go soaring.

U.S. News & World Report. 76:57-8. My. 27, '74. In the end, even U.S. may not be able to feed the world.

*U.S. News & World Report. 77:87-90. N. 18, '74. As famine spreads—what's to be done.

U.S. News & World Report. 77:20-2. D. 16, '74. Hot debate: what U.S. owes to the world's hungry.

U.S. News & World Report. 78:24-6. Ja. 6, '75. Food prices—why Butz sees rise easing in year ahead; interview.

U.S. News & World Report. 78:24-6. Mr. 24, '75. Enough food to feed the world, if—.

U.S. News & World Report. 78:27-8. Mr. 24, '75. Why Russia still has trouble feeding itself. J. N. Wallace.

*U.S. News & World Report. 78:74. Ap. 21, '75. Fish farming—it's catching on.

UNESCO Courier. 27:4-6. Jl. '74. We the undersigned: declaration on food and population.

UNESCO Courier. 27:7-12. Jl. '74. Can the earth feed the growing multitudes? Roger Revelle.

UNESCO Courier. 27:13-18. Jl. '74. World gone mad. René Dumont.

*UNICEF's World. No. 1102:2. '74. What can UNICEF do?

Vital Speeches of the Day. 39:403-5. Ap. 15, '73. Will world population outstrip food supplies? address, February 20, 1973. Colin Clark.

Vital Speeches of the Day. 39:465-7. My. 15, '73. Food, farm programs, and the future; address, April 3, 1973. E. L. Butz.

Vital Speeches of the Day. 40:28-32. O. 15, '73. Can the world afford to feed itself? address, June 27, 1973. G. W. Thomas.

Vital Speeches of the Day. 40:197-9. Ja. 15, '74. Realistic look at food reserves; address, December 11, 1973. E. L. Butz.

Vital Speeches of the Day. 40:405-8. Ap. 15, '74. Tyranny of hunger; address, March 11, 1974. R. E. Anderson.
Vital Speeches of the Day. 41:13-20. O. 15, '74. Third world: millions facing risk of death; address, September 30, 1974. R. S. McNamara.
Vital Speeches of the Day. 41:202-5. Ja. 15, '75. Great race: farmers throughout the world; address, December 8, 1974. H. C. Jacobs.
Wall Street Journal. p 36. Jl. 26, '73. Parson Malthus, revisited. Robert Keatley.
Wall Street Journal. p 14. S. 14, '73. The growing threat of world famine. R. L. Prosterman.
Wall Street Journal. p 1+. O. 9, 10, 15, 23, 31, '73. Land of plenty (series). J. A. Prestbo and others.
Wall Street Journal. p 28. O. 10, '73. The need for a world food reserve. L. R. Brown.
Wall Street Journal. p 1+. O. 3, 8, 11, 23, N. 11, 18, D. 3, '74. Food crisis (series). Mary Bralove and others.
Wall Street Journal. p 1+. D. 18, '74. The food crisis: new-food research isn't likely to ease poor nations' hunger. David Brand.
Wall Street Journal. p 8. Ja. 20, '75. Food, famine and ideology. Irving Kristol.
*War on Hunger. 8:5-8. Je. '74. Fertilizer "panic." D. C. McCune.
*War on Hunger. 8:1-2. O. '74. A "special responsibility." G. R. Ford.
*War on Hunger. 8:1-4+. D. '74. No child will go to bed hungry. Henry Kissinger.
*War on Hunger. 9:1-4+. F. '75. State of man. Philip Handler.
War on Hunger. 9:9-12. Mr. '75. Question of independence. Helen Nash.
*Washington Post. p 1+. Mr. 9-14, '75. Food aid business.
Reprinted in this book: Food aid role weighed. Washington Post. p 1+. Mr. 14, '75. Dan Morgan.
World. 2:30+. My. 22, '73. Greening of India. D. S. Connery.